WHAT'S WITH THE DUDES AT THE DOOR?

Books by Kevin Johnson

Early Teen Devotionals

Can I Be a Christian Without Being Weird?
Could Someone Wake Me Up Before I Drool on the Desk?
Does Anybody Know What Planet My Parents Are From?
So Who Says I Have to Act My Age?
Who Should I Listen To?
Why Can't My Life Be a Summer Vacation?
Why Is God Looking for Friends?

Books for Teens

Catch the Wave!
Find Your Fit (with Jane A. G. Kise)
Look Who's Toast Now!
What's With the Dudes at the Door?

To find out more about Kevin Johnson's books,
visit his Web site: www.thewave.org

Books by James White

The Forgotten Trinity
Grieving: Our Path Back to Peace
Is the Mormon My Brother?
The King James Only Controversy
Letters to a Mormon Elder
The Roman Catholic Controversy

To find out more about James White's books,
visit his website: www.aomin.org

Kevin JOHNSON & James WHITE

WHAT'S WITH THE DUDES AT THE DOOR?

BETHANY HOUSE PUBLISHERS
MINNEAPOLIS, MINNESOTA 55438

What's With the Dudes at the Door?
Copyright © 1998
Kevin Walter Johnson and James White

Cover illustration by Scott Angle
Cover design by The Lookout Design Group

Published by Bethany House Publishers
A Ministry of Bethany Fellowship International
11300 Hampshire Avenue South
Minneapolis, Minnesota 55438

Printed in the United States of America by
Bethany Press International, Minneapolis, Minnesota 55438

Library of Congress Cataloging-in-Publication Data

CIP data applied for

ISBN 0-7642-2070-5   CIP

To Steve Laube
Great friend, wonderful editor, all-around nice guy,
and fellow chicken aficionado.

KEVIN JOHNSON joined Bethany House Publishers as a senior editor after five years as associate pastor for more than four hundred sixth through ninth graders at Elmbrook Church in metro Milwaukee. He is the bestselling author of half a dozen early teen devotionals as well as books for youth on missions and the end times.

JAMES WHITE is director of ministries for *Alpha and Omega Ministries*, a Christian apologetics organization based in Phoenix, Arizona, and an adjunct professor with Golden Gate Baptist Theological Seminary's Arizona Campus. He is also professor of Apologetics with Columbia Evangelical Seminary, and a critical consultant for the Lockman Foundation on the *New American Standard Bible* update.

CONTENTS

"Test everything.
Hold on
to the good.
Avoid every kind
of evil."

—1 Thessalonians 5:21-22

chapter 1

You've Got Dudes Dinging Your Doorbell

Saturday chores. What a bore. You slave all week at school, then work all weekend, too. If you had your druthers you'd have slept half the day. Instead, you got up and got at it. But now—with the bathrooms scrubbed, your bedroom sort of spotless, and the garage swept out—you've earned a hassle-free flop in front of the TV for an afternoon game.

Popcorn.

Pop.

Remote.

You're ready.

DING-DONG! Your dad glances at you with his you-get-it-because-it's-always-for-you look. You groan and roll off the couch. Who'd ding the doorbell on a Saturday?

You open the door to see two guys. Each sports a tie. (A tie? On Saturday? Isn't that illegal?) And a black name badge. Your dad follows you to the door—you can't figure out why—and he's not looking overly happy. He pushes in front of you. He grunts at the strangers.

"Hello," one of them begins. "We're out this afternoon

sharing a message about families and how important they are. And how you can keep them together for eternity."

Your dad seems to sigh. He must know where this is headed. But you don't. What sort of dudes dress up and knock on doors to talk about stuff like this?

"Wouldn't you agree," they continue, "that we live in difficult times? And wouldn't you say that the family is under constant attack?"

Hey, you think, Dad said that just last night at dinner. Your pastor says the same thing on Sunday mornings, too. You notice that one of the guys has flipped out a Bible—well, it *looks* like a Bible—and is opening to a passage.

"Look, I'm really not interested," your dad says, exasperated. You're a little surprised. Dad knows the Bible pretty well, and he isn't shy to talk about God. He's always helping at church. He and Mom make sure you're there a couple times a week. He even prayed with you to ask Jesus to forgive your sins. So why isn't he interested in talking to these guys—aside from the fact that he's wearing nasty old sweats? And that they interrupted his game?

"But wouldn't you agree that knowing God's truth about these final days is vitally important for you and your family?" one of the guys asks. They don't give up. "And we have a message to bring you from God. He has given us another testament of Jesus Christ, called the Book of—"

"Yes, I know," your dad replies. "I know who you are, and I'm not interested in your literature, or your books of Scripture, or whatever else you have to offer. Maybe *you* would consider joining *us* tomorrow morning at *our* church. Then we could talk."

The guy holding the Bible shuts it and tucks it under his

arm. "Well, if you ever wish to know more about Christ's restored Church in these last days, I hope you will look us up. Have a good day!" And with that, they turn and leave.

You go back to the game. Yet you can't shake the image of those two dudes. They seemed so confident. You wouldn't be so brave standing at a stranger's door with your Bible in your hand! And why did your dad turn them away?

Your dad settles back down in his chair. The game has cut to a commercial.

"So, Dad, who were those guys, anyhow?"

"Oh, just some LDS."

"LDS? What's that?"

"Latter-day Saints. Mormons. They're known by various names. They're members of a cult."

CULT? They didn't *look* like cultists. No shaved heads, no flowers to sell, no glassy-eyed chanting. Cult?

"Why are they a cult?" you ask.

"Well, they teach things that aren't true. They don't believe in the Trinity, and they have some strange beliefs about becoming gods themselves someday."

You remember hearing something about this stuff in church a long time ago. But you hadn't paid much attention. Now something is bugging you.

"But they had a Bible with them, and they didn't say anything you haven't said, and—"

Whoops. Dad doesn't like that. "There's more to it than that," he shoots back. "They're trained to use the Bible to teach *their* doctrines. But they're *mis*using the Bible. They're not using it the way they should. If you want to know more about them, talk to Pastor Evenson tomorrow. He can really clear things up for you."

11

Snakes Slithering in Your Yard

You probably don't wonder if Bigfoot lives in your backyard. You know better. You know he doesn't exist.

That doesn't mean, however, that you know *everything* that lives in your yard. No doubt you could skim a pile of nature guidebooks and spot all sorts of species that *might* be there. And just because you haven't seen them doesn't mean they *aren't*.

Get this fact about what lives in the big backyard of your world: There are, counting conservatively, many millions of cult members in North America alone. Notice it or not, they're knocking on your door. They tromp through your neighborhood. They invite you to youth group activities and campus Bible studies. Their churches might occupy a prominent corner in your neighborhood. The largest cults run ads on network TV, and most are all over the Web.

So cults are closer than you might have thunk.

Another backyard lesson: You don't need to know the names of all sixteen brands of mosquitoes out back that make your summer evenings miserable. Or the twelve different songbirds that warble you awake. But if your yard was fence-to-fence with deadly snakes, you'd want to know. You'd want to know all about the ones that wrap around your neck, that drop from trees, that gnaw you to nothing. Or murder you with one fang.

And get this: Cults are deadly. They hold beliefs that are counterfeits of true Christianity. They follow fake faiths. Goofed-up gospels. Cult members may be superhumanly religious, but they don't know the real God of Christianity.

So you'd better know how to spot them.

Maybe you wouldn't recognize a cultist if he stood on your doorstep. Maybe you can't tell the difference between real Christianity and the bogus faiths of the cults. Maybe you haven't realized the spiritual danger of cultic teaching.

That doesn't mean cults don't slither in the grass.

That doesn't make their bites any less spiritually deadly.

The Ones That Squeeze Around Your Neck

Almost everyone gets upset by weirdo cults you hear about on the news—the ones that more or less kidnap people and vacuum out their brains. You'd expect folks to frown on that. But what about those guys on your step? What's the harm in them? They seem like they just want to chat about God. Sure, they sound persuasive. But they also sound like vacuum cleaner salesmen—the harmless *vroom-vroom-get-the-dirt-out-of-your-carpet* kind, not the hazardous brain-suctioning kind.

If that's what you think, think again—while you still possess your brain.

Cults far out-witness most Christians. We try to tell people about our faith. They *aggressively* persuade people to adopt theirs. Take this true example of a Jehovah's Witness named Andrea and a Christian named Miguel.

Scene 1: A church asks Miguel, a countercult worker, to talk with Karen, who's started studying the Bible with Jehovah's Witnesses. In a sort of spiritual showdown, Karen seats Miguel across the kitchen table from Andrea. When Andrea tries to clobber Miguel with Greek—the original language of the New Testament—Miguel swats down Andrea's arguments point-by-point. By the end of the evening,

13

Andrea gets abusive ("What rock did you dig this guy out from underneath?!"). Karen sees what is what and stops studying with the Witnesses.

Scene 2: The next year Miguel gets another call from the same church. A guy named Ryan is studying with JWs. Guess *which* JWs? Andrea and her husband. But by the end of an evening with Miguel, Ryan is ready to share his newfound knowledge with the Witnesses.

Scene 3: Andrea is down but not out. A few months later Miguel sees a bunch of young Witnesses doing door-to-door witnessing close to his own house. Miguel is having a polite chat with them when suddenly up comes a big van. Guess who pops out? Andrea. She herds her students into the van and drives down the road. But they park in the wrong spot and meet up with Miguel again as he's out for a walk. Andrea's young Witnesses protest to Miguel: "You didn't tell us you're a former Witness!"

"That's because I'm not," Miguel replies. He walks over to the passenger window of the van and knocks. *Whhhhrrrr.* Down comes the window. The young Witnesses hear an earful. "Andrea," Miguel asks, "is telling a lie still a sin for Witnesses? You know I'm not a former Witness. So why did you lie to those young people?" *Whhhhrrrr.* Up goes the window. Off speeds the van.

Species: Cultus Notsoanonymous

Mormons and Jehovah's Witnesses are the two largest counterfeit Christian groups in the world. But not the only ones. A wild variety of creatures likely live in a backyard near you. Here's a small selection of biggie cults you're most likely to see:

- *Mormons* or *Latter-day Saints* are probably some of the dudes at your door. They're usually moral, family-oriented people. You might look at your LDS classmates and feel like you're looking in a mirror—they're a lot like you. But Mormonism teaches that God was once a man—not that God was born as a man in Jesus, but that God was once a run-of-the-mill human who was promoted to Godhood. They teach, too, that men can become gods. And that a huge swarm of gods populate the universe.

- *Jehovah's Witnesses* also take religion door-to-door, passing out literature that often focuses on end-of-the-world and society-is-going-to-hell-in-a-hand-basket themes. JWs are the nice kids at school who sit out holidays and birthdays. Their big problem is that they don't believe Jesus is fully God. Like the Mormons, they probably have a church somewhere near you.

- *Christian Scientists* likely run a "Reading Room" in a storefront or strip mall near you. Known for distributing literature, they also own the prestigious *Christian Science Monitor* newspaper and the on-again, off-again *Monitor Radio*. They do great reporting on international happenings—but awful reporting on God. They say he's a mere "principle" or "mind"—not a personal God.

- *Unitarian-Universalists* embrace a hodgepodge of spiritualities. But they can sound Christian enough to fool you. An intellectual bunch, Unitarian-Universalists are often well represented on university faculties.

- *The Way* is a small but aggressive group you'll spot on college campuses inviting students to Bible studies. They don't, of course, hang out a sign proclaiming that they aren't true Christians. (Don't get them confused with solid Christian groups on campus like InterVarsity Christian Fellowship, the Navigators, Campus Crusade, International Students Incorporated, or ChiAlpha.) Like Jehovah's Witnesses, followers of The Way don't believe Jesus is God. They insist you speak in tongues. And they think all other Christians are absolutely corrupt.

■ The *Boston Church* or *International Churches of Christ* claims to hold to historical Christian beliefs. They're tidy, spiritually intense people sincerely bent on spiritual maturity. In reality, however, they seem to teach that to be a real Christian you have to be baptized and discipled by them—and remain a part of their group. Fed-up ex-members say their methods are mind controlling. The ICoC is extremely active on college campuses.

Tuck this mini-catalog of cults in your brain as you look around your town. You might be surprised what you spot in your own backyard.

What's worse, that list doesn't even touch the small, way-out-there wacko cults you see on CNN. David Koresh and his *Branch Davidians*—the cult from Waco that held the FBI at bay and then went up in smoke. *Heaven's Gaters*—the California group that tried to catch a ride on a spaceship supposedly stashed in the tail of Comet Hale-Bopp. *People's Temple*—most of whom died in a massacre in Jonestown, Guyana. *Aum Shinrikyo*—a largish cult that blew Nazi-invented nerve gas through the Tokyo subway system.

These obscure, radical cults are relatively few and far be-

16

tween. And by the time that kind of cult makes the news, they've usually self-destructed. (Remember this, though: They all start somewhere. Maybe in a neighborhood near you. And somehow they get people to buy their hostile, violent view of the world. Moral of the story: Don't sell your soul to the kid three houses away who prays to squirrels— then pan-fries them.)

The Cult-Proofed You

Cults aren't going to go away. They aren't content to hide under the backyard tool shed and snakepile to themselves.

Cults endanger you. What cults teach, spiritually speaking, is an eternal enchilada short of a Tex-Mex combo. Get a hold of this blunt truth: Their message of how to know God leads people away from true saving faith. To a savior other than Jesus. In the other direction from heaven. What might seem like a what's-the-big-deal? issue to us actually decides whether someone is in the Kingdom or not. For now. And forever.

You face a two-pronged danger. Learn this lesson from *Star Trek*: Two things can kill you when you say, "Beam me up, Scotty." First, Scotty might lock you onto the wrong coordinates and beam you into ferociously hot lava in the interior of the third rock from the sun Kolob. That would be bad. Second, you would also die if the dilithium—as Scotty would say—*roons oot*, the Enterprise powers down, and Scotty loses you in transmission. You'd never rematerialize.

In plain English: Your faith needs to be clear and strong so that you don't land in a cult. But just as important, your faith needs to be powerful enough to avoid getting between belief systems. A cult *may* not persuade you to follow their faith, but they might be one of many forces in life that wears you down and convinces you to chuck your faith and thumb a big "Who Needs It!" at Christianity, convinced that no one has the real truth about God.

You don't want to get sucked in.

You don't want to get stuck.

A Cult-Proofed World

Getting *you* cult-proofed is the biggie priority of *What's With the Dudes at the Door?* You'll find out

- What makes a cult a cult
- Why you need to stick to what you believe
- What real Christianity teaches
- How cults miss that standard

But getting those things figured out accomplishes one more thing. It readies you to start sharing your real God with real people caught in real cults—especially friends who need the truth. Bashing the people caught in cults isn't the goal of this book. The aim is uncovering true faith for your sake and theirs.

You can shoo cultists off your step—and miss the chance to meet them on your own turf. You could choose to ignore cultists and hope they go away—but they always come back. You could stupidly get in a fist fight over faith—and share a cell with a cultist for a few years. Fleeing a chance to share—or forcing someone to faith—is *never* how God operates. Sooner or later you have to reckon with cults' claims.

God has a better way of dealing with the cults. It's the same tack he wants us to take toward anyone who doesn't know him. Paul put it this way to Timothy:

> Don't have anything to do with foolish and stupid arguments, because you know they produce quarrels. And the Lord's servant must not quarrel; instead, he must be kind to everyone, able to teach, not resentful. Those who oppose him he must gently instruct, in the hope that God will grant them repentance leading them to a knowledge of the truth, and that they will come to their senses and escape from the trap of the devil, who has taken them captive to do his will. (2 Timothy 2:23–26)

"Don't have stupid arguments" assumes you aren't stupid. You understand what you claim to believe. "Must not quarrel" means you keep your cool, being kind to everyone. You "gently instruct." And you do everything with hope that "God will grant [people] repentance leading them to a knowledge of the truth."

Saving yourself from cults sounds scary. But necessary.

Saving other people sounds staggering. Veritably overwhelming.

But think about this: Paul wrote those words to Timothy, who had functioned as a pastor since he was sixteen. Tim was still young. And imperfect. Paul's words immediately before the passage clipped above remind Timothy to "flee the evil desires of youth, and pursue righteousness, faith, love and peace, along with those who call on the Lord out of a pure heart" (2 Timothy 2:22).

Timothy was still growing. But God thought he could be

smart. Keep his cool. Gently instruct. And help people escape fake faith.

He thinks the same thing about you.

Any questions?

How about this one: *How do you tell real faith from fake faith?*

Think About This Stuff:

1. Why does it matter that you know how to spot the unbiblical teaching of the cults?
2. Which of the cults briefly described in this chapter have you heard of? Are they active in your area? Are any of your friends members of cults?
3. What two dangers do cults pose to you as a Christian?
4. How do you and your family react when dudes come knocking at your door?

"You shall have no other gods before me."

—Exodus 20:3

Some of the Sweetest People Are Cultists

chapter 2

Timewarp back a few decades.

Picture yourself in a crustified high school cafeteria.

Plop down in that land of lunchroom-tables-not-long-ago and ponder your surroundings: Almost everyone at your table goes to church. They believe in the same God—or know they should. Most label themselves Christian. Or Jews. The few who break the mold keep quiet.

Not anymore.

A present-day glance around your school lunchroom likely shows friends and classmates who munch on all sorts of spiritualities. One girl says she doesn't need a building to worship God. She communes with nature, and the pretty rock around her neck fills her with power. Other friends— well, they're into bug-free, indoor worship. But not in any church. One friend goes to a mosque. He prays several times a day. Another guy is pumped to go on a two-year mission for his Mormon church. Another friend burns incense under a temple roof full of little guys who look like they're in an ugly mood—no Bible in sight, no set day or time to show up. She reveres multiple gods, spiritual entities with a small *g*. And then there's you.

If you're lucky, everybody finds a way to get along.

But that doesn't mean what everybody believes is true.

Choosing Your Religion

Know it or not, we all have a religion. We all believe something. Even the big mob of students who aren't clear on what they believe still have answers to questions they don't even know they've asked. When it comes to faith, we all face some no-compromise, pick-one-or-the-other choices. And our answers define what we believe.

First choice: Do you believe in *God* or *No God*?

Some people live in a WYSIWYG world. They think *What You See Is What You Get*. If they can't see it, smell it, or measure it, then it doesn't exist. Since God is invisible, odor-free, and impossible to wrap in a tape measure, they refuse to believe in him. Some of these people call themselves *atheists*, convinced that nothing around us indicates God is real. Others call themselves *agnostics*, admitting that God may exist but claiming we can't figure him out.

A bigger chunk of the human race, however, thinks there's more to this world than what meets the eye. Lurking just beyond this planet and the plants, animals, and people who fill it, they say, is a force that made it all happen. So what is that something? Or is it a some*one*?

Next choice: Do you believe in the *God of the Bible* or *some other god*?

Christians explain that we exist because the all-powerful God of the Bible made us. Others say the world was whipped

24

into shape by an impersonal force. Or that the planet is run by a collection of lesser gods, smaller spiritual beings.

Some people try to add other religions to Christianity. That's like sloshing up a bladder-buster-sized soda at a quik-mart. When you mix too many flavors at the fountain, the slop in your cup is called a *suicide*. When you try to blend together Christian faith with other faiths of the world and pretend differences don't exist, the muck in your brain is called *syncretism*—a mixing and matching of different faiths.

It doesn't take a load of logic to figure out that God can't be an impersonal force *and* a knowable, personal being. Or that there could be one God *and* a gaggle of gods. Or that we can be made right with God by the death of Jesus *and* by our own efforts to behave. When we recognize what religions really teach, we see they present us with an either-or decision. We can't be a Christian *and* a Muslim, Hindu, Buddhist, or New Ager.

Third choice: Do you believe *Jesus makes us right with God* or *We need Jesus-plus-something-else?*

It isn't hard to spot the differences between a Christian and an atheist. Or between a Buddhist and a Bible believer. But this third question gets sticky and tricky. Multitudes of people act and smell Christian yet deny the core truths that make Christianity what it is. These people all claim to be Christians. They're all way off.

What's With the Dudes at the Door? doesn't struggle to prove God exists. That's a crucial point—but that's the realm of biblical answers to *philosophies* and *isms*. It doesn't sort through how Christianity differs from the faith systems of the world. That's a study of *comparative religions*. This book looks at *cults*—the variety of groups that twist and distort Christian faith. We'll see why their beliefs can't be called Christian. And why it matters.

Knock the "T" off Tolerant

Cult. It's a nasty term. It fills your head with images of David Koresh igniting Waco. Jim Jones spiking juice with cyanide. Heaven's Gate Bopponauts lying dead in their new Nikes, waiting to hitch a spaceship ride to a higher existence.

Understandably, people take it hard if you call them a "cultist" or their beliefs "cultic." In fact, people nowadays want to string you up by your First-Amendment-protected vocal cords if you suggest that they are in any way *wrong*. Posters on one campus put it this way: "It isn't wrong to think you're right. But it's wrong to think others are wrong."

Especially when it comes to religion, if you dare claim you know ultimate, total truth, you might as well wear a sign that says, "KICK ME. I'M INTOLERANT." You're labeled arrogant, offensive, and unloving.

Big problem.

Christians are to be all-loving. That's different, however, from all-inclusive, all-accepting, all-tolerant. Anyone who has read even a few paragraphs of the Bible knows that God purports to have revealed through his Word what's true and what's not.

He says that he alone is God—which means no one else gets to wear "God" on his name tag.

He says that we can know him through Christ alone—which means no other Lord will do.

He tells us how we should follow him—which means he alone is smart enough to make the rules for life.

God gets mighty hung up on how we talk about him. He put some pretty strong words in the Bible for false teachings and for false teachers (2 Peter 2:1–9; Matthew 7:15–16; 2 Corinthians 11:13–15; 1 Timothy 1:3–4, 6:3–5; 1 John 4:1). So what's a Christian to do?

A Line in the Sand

In the days before the Gulf War in the early 1990s, George Bush gave enemies of the allied coalition an ultimatum. After the Iraqis invaded Kuwait, the President of the United States warned Saddam Hussein and his troops to go no farther. He "drew a line in the sand." No one misunderstood what he meant: *Cross that line, you die.*

The line was *necessary*. It marked the division between oppression and freedom. It set life on one side, dictatorship and death squads on the other. The line was *clear*. Bush did everything but drag his toe through the sand to demonstrate what he meant.

Christians who want a faith that works—for themselves, for their friends, and for the planet—have a mondo line to draw. Our goal isn't to bump off the people who stand on the wrong side of the line, to get physical with them the way an army takes on an enemy. Our goal is to understand what separates true Christianity from counterfeits. It's to point the way to spiritual life and warn of spiritual death. If we're going to know what makes a cult a cult, we have to know how to separate fake from real.

"Cult" can mean a lot of things. Some definitions apply to practically everyone. If a cult is "a group of people dedicated to the teachings of a particular religious leader," then all Christians are cultists because we follow the teachings of Jesus. If we widen the definition to include "people dedicated to a cause—those with a great willingness to sacrifice time, possessions, even life," again, you are a cultist.

It's obvious that "cult" means nothing if we don't define it carefully. It's almost easier, in fact, to start with what it *doesn't* mean than what it *does*.

Everybodybutus isn't the name of a cult.

Some Christians toss "cult" around so lightly that they make it sound like everyone in California—make that everyone outside *their* little group—belongs to a cult. Anyone who doesn't follow their exact recipe for what it means to be a Christian is a sinister cultist out to get them. It's not a fun way to view the world, and it's not a helpful way to look at cults.

Anti-God beliefs don't make someone a cultist.

There are all sorts of "isms" out there that—laid side by side with the Bible—are as wrong as wrong gets. Their ways of thinking are directly opposed to God and Christ. Our world, for instance, is soaked in a viewpoint known as "naturalistic materialism." It's that belief mentioned a couple pages back—the atheistic one that says the only stuff that is real is what you find in nature, that there's no spiritual realm, and that everything in the world came about by natural processes. It's mistaken because it leaves out God, but it's not *cultic*.

Alternate-god beliefs aren't what makes a cult.

Your neighbors who follow the teachings of other religions aren't cultists. They make no claim to heed the Bible. They declare no loyalty to Christ. They openly admit they worship something other than the Christian's God. They are followers of other, often ancient, religions. They need to know Jesus, but they aren't members of the cult club.

Blow the Whistle on Intramural Squabbles

Those first three items on our "not a cult" list have to do with how we see non-Christians. But what about groups that claim to be Christian? Remember, that's where differences get harder to discern. Not everything you think is weird or wrong, though, is worth having a cult-sized cow over.

Different styles of Christian faith doth not a cult make.

If you haven't hung out in a lot of churches, you might be downright uncomfortable visiting another church—even one a friend goes to. They might seem to do everything differently. And because it's common to define "right" by how *you* do things, you might be tempted to think "different" means "wrong."

God isn't so uptight. He allows us to have differences in many areas. He doesn't tell us how to do everything at church. Because we aren't clones, we worship the same God in somewhat different ways. Do you worship God on Sunday

29

or Saturday? For some, that's a big issue. What does the pastor wear—a robe, a suit, or baggy shorts and a loud Hawaiian shirt? Do you even have a pastor? Is the service lit up with candles—or do you dislike smells and bells? Does a choir sing? Do you listen to organ, piano—or fuzzed, phased, and chorused guitar riffs? Do you stand up, sit down, kneel—or keep your portable, personal padding more or less permanently planted in the pew?

Christians disagree in wads of ways. Sometimes their differences are so deep that they can't get along. Churches split. New clumps of churches—denominations—group and regroup. Chances are your own church has watched a number of members leave in a huff. The arguments may be heated and the parting painful, but these disagreements are rarely over things that *define* the Christian faith. They don't make anyone a cultist.

Different beliefs don't necessarily make a group a cult.

Huh? Isn't countercult stuff basically a fight for what we *believe*?

Doctrine—what a church teaches about Christian faith—is surely important to discuss and study. It even divides us into different churches and different denominations (it makes us Baptist, Lutheran, Presbyterian, Methodist, "non-denominational," or a countless variety of other things). Not *all* doctrine, though, is at the core of what it means to be a Christian. How, when, and why to baptize energizes many churches today. Churches form around differing understandings of spiritual gifts and how to get holy. Emotions rev high over the timing of Christ's return. These are vital things, light-years removed from insignificant details like the color of the stripes in your church's parking lot. But most folks admit that when it comes down to "Is this person *Christian* in their beliefs?" the sane answer is still "Of course!"

Spotting the Real Thing

You shouldn't give up trying to find answers on big topics that divide Christians. You don't want to defend what you believe simply because it's what you're used to or because it feels better. You want to hold traditions lightly and the Bible tightly.

But the blunt truth is that so far none of these differences between Christians is what *makes you a Christian*—or keeps you out of God's favor. Just because we disagree doesn't mean one of us is headed for the glowing fires of hell. It's easy to make minor points of faith major. Christians who disagree aren't cultists. We're stubborn.

To really get a handle on the term "cult," we need to distinguish between what beliefs *define* the Christian faith and what beliefs *don't*. Of course, lots of Christians argue about which things belong on which list. But most folks now and in the past have agreed that there are a handful of things you can't do without—the most basic points of Christian belief.

Cults 101

Here's the puzzle: If we can disagree on all sorts of issues and still be Christian—still be "saved," still enjoy God's grace and forgiveness in Christ—what's with all the fuss over cults?

That has to do with some true/false questions on God's Great Final Exam. Not everything in the Christian faith is open to interpretation. And God has a few questions he expects you to answer correctly. They're questions you can't miss—or you fail the test. These are the issues that *God himself* says are must-know, don't-blow-this-on-the-exam kind of things.

Here's the kicker: There are entire groups that insist their wrong answers are right. Not out of ignorance, but on purpose. These groups claim to have a new answer key, one never seen before their particular founder came along. Give their answers on these central questions, follow their leadership, go through their program, and you're in with God. Reject their particular way and you are permanently out.

And that's how we can define not just what a cult *isn't* but what a cult *is*.

> A cult is a group that claims to be Christian—often claiming that they *alone* are the true Christian Church—but denies the core teachings that define the Christian faith.

Read that a few times. While there are many *signs* of a cult, this is what really *defines* such a group. They may teach that God came from another planet (the Mormons), that only 144,000 people will enjoy heaven (Jehovah's Witnesses), or that their leader has the right to slip children deadly cyanide (People's Temple), but this is where the mayhem starts. They claim to be Christian. They claim their group is worthy to wear that high name. Yet when it comes to the very doctrines that *define the faith itself* and separate Christianity from all other religions, they refuse to believe them and insist on some other belief. You'll notice that this definition doesn't include *all* the scary religious groups in the world, but it might include the nice people next door. This definition focuses on *counterfeits of the Christian faith.*

So what are these whopper doctrines about which cults teach whopper untruths? Some anti-cult researchers have a pretty full list. The beliefs of cultic groups stray so far from Christianity—some subtly, some wildly—that a catalog of wacko beliefs would occupy thousands of pages. The real problem, though, is that cults are messed up on three teachings central to Christianity:

1. Who God is
2. What God has done in Jesus
3. How we know (the Bible)

Why these three beliefs? Think about it. These are things at the very core of what we believe.

The Greatness of Who God Is

One of the extreme goals of the Christian life is that we get to know God. The Bible specifically warns over and over that messed-up people will try to lead us away from true understanding of who God is. One example:

> Therefore, dear friends, since you already know this, be on your guard so that you may not be carried away by the error of lawless men and fall from your secure po-

sition. But grow in the grace and knowledge of our Lord and Savior Jesus Christ. To him be glory both now and forever! Amen. (2 Peter 3:17–18)

God gets glory when we *know him*. We won't gawk at his greatness when we are deceived about him. We won't praise his purposes if we misunderstand them. We won't follow with wild joy when we hate his commands.

The Bible shows that God is truly down on idolatry—worshiping something other than him. In fact, the first commandment is "You shall have no other Gods before me" (Exodus 20:3). Why? Because idolatry *always* leads people *away* from him. How would you like it if people constantly lied about you, telling others you're something you're really not? And what if you had to watch people misinterpret and dislike you based on a pack of falsehoods? That's what teaching false things about God does. It's lying about God.

Serious stuff.

God's Mind-Boggling Work in Jesus

God sent his Son into this world to bring sinners back to himself. If it's the most important thing God is up to, it should be important to us, too. Who Jesus *is*—fully God, fully human—is really important. What he *did*—dying to bring us back to God—is really important, too. When people say that Jesus really can't save anyone or that he can only save us when we add our own works or "merit" to what he does, that messes with how God says we can know him. If you want to really see how dangerously important this is and how bad it is to mess with the Gospel (God's "Good News" about how Jesus saves us), peek at this:

I am astonished that you are so quickly deserting the one who called you by the grace of Christ and are turning to a different gospel—which is really no gospel at all. Evidently some people are throwing you into confusion and are trying to pervert the gospel of Christ. But even if we or an angel from heaven should preach a gospel other than the one we preached to you, *let him be eternally condemned!* As we have already said, so now I say again: If anybody is preaching to you a gospel other than what you accepted, *let him be eternally condemned!* (Galatians 1:6–9, italics added)

There's even more astonishing stuff in Galatians 3:1–4 and 5:7–12. Christians believe that God makes people right with him through Jesus Christ, who *alone* is the Way, the Truth, and the Life (John 14:6). That makes it ultra-important to get the message straight about what God has done in Jesus.

Take It on God's Word

If you want to mess with the Christian faith, mess with the Bible. Christianity is based on what God has told us there.

Start playing with the Bible and you'll be in real deep trouble. Take away or add stuff and you'll soon completely botch the message. Or if you really want to be tricky, you can start mistranslating the Bible—which was written long before *Beowulf* or anything remotely resembling the English language. Hence the need for good translations so we can know God's truth. All cults have ways of messing with the Word, and it always leads to false teachings.

Paul told Timothy, "Continue in what you have learned and have become convinced of, because you know those from whom you learned it, and how from infancy you have known the holy Scriptures, which are able to make you wise for salvation through faith in Christ Jesus" (2 Timothy 3:14–15). The Bible reveals Christ, and Christ reveals God. And that true knowledge of God is what allows us to know him as he really is.

Again, pretty necessary stuff.

God Is No Build-Your-Own Tostada Bar

Get this: God won't let the human race treat him like a build-your-own tostada bar. You can't pick the guacamole but flick the onions, or choose the cheese but lose the beans, making God fit your taste. It's *never* okay to make God into what you think best—not to invent your own religion, not to grab one from a group that creates gods and religions different from what the true God has revealed of himself in the Bible. God wants us to know him exactly as he is—as he's shown himself to be.

Truth brings life. Lies bring death. Cults bring spiritual death to those who cling to their misshaped gods.

It's tempting to waffle on truth.

God won't.

It's easy to be tolerant, never speak bad, never say anyone is wrong about anything.

God is kind. But he isn't so shy.

Think About This Stuff:

1. Explain the three choices all people make about issues of faith.

2. Why can't Christians accept what cults teach? What's the difference between being intolerant and unloving?
3. What things *don't* make someone a cultist?
4. How does *What's With the Dudes at the Door?* define "cult"? What three beliefs are big in that definition? Why?

"Contend for the faith that was once for all entrusted to the saints."

—Jude 1:3

Can't We All Just Get Along?

chapter **3**

David's face wore that boy-yanked-by-ear look. He stared at the floor, embarrassed he'd been dragged to his pastor's office. David's mom sat him down right next to the gnarled old clergy guy. Intimidating—and an easy grab if the pastor decided to reach out and strangle him.

For David's pastor, the situation was nothing new. Boy meets girl. Boy falls in love with girl. Boy shocks family by suddenly announcing he's been baptized at girl's church—a *Mormon* church—and signed up for a two-year mission. Parents of boy cry. Boy protests: His girl is the most beauteous woman in the world—he'd die without her—she's made it ultra-obvious that she'll only marry a Mormon boy who has served his mission for the Church—*blah blah* more excuses *blah blah*. Boy knows what he needs to do. Join up. Do mission.

So *then* Mom calls pastor—when boy is way gone—a move akin to calling a plumber after your retainer has dropped in the toilet *and* been flushed halfway to the Pacific.

"David," the pastor began, "if you joined the LDS

Church because you've decided you share their beliefs, we have a lot to talk about. I can show you some things to help you rethink what you're doing. But if your hormones are the reason you joined, I can't help you. We'll be wasting our time here today."

David huffed a *Who, me?* face. He was doubly shocked. First, his pastor knew and had correctly used the word "hormones." Second, someone was calling his bluff.

He mumbled that he really did believe the LDS Church was the one true church.

The conversation crumbled.

David went on his mission.

His girlfriend married someone else while he was gone. *Gotcha.*

Freedom to Choose—and to Lose

It's doubtful that David ever slowly, sanely mulled whether he should date an LDS girl. What's to wonder about? She's moral, smart, and gorgeous. What a total package! (Nothing more to buy—whoops, did the salesgal mention that "new religion thingy" buried in the fine print?) Yeah, David had heard Mormons believe some strange things, but his brain back-burnered that. He'd also heard his youth pastor talk about not being "unequally yoked with unbelievers" (2 Corinthians 6:14–17). But that didn't have anything to do with *dating*, did it? Besides, she said she was a Christian.

What's the big deal? Why shouldn't David date or even marry a sweet Mormon girl? Why can't we all just get along?

David is entitled to believe whatever he wants.

So is his Mormon gal friend. So are you. God gives each person freedom to choose his way or the run-away-from-him highway.

Everyone has freedom to believe *whatever*. That doesn't mean everyone is right. Or that the All-Wise God of Everything agrees. Or that every life-choice is beneficial to the chooser.

So what's the big deal?

Well, David's life has never been the same. He charged down a road he and everyone who cares about him wishes he hadn't. David let a cutie put a ring in his nose and tow him where he shouldn't have gone. He let himself be blinded by love. Which is fun only till you put an eye out. Or snuff your soul.

Baiting a Trap—For You

Dating in the Danger Zone isn't the only way to fall into a cult. Truth is, you don't even have to try. The cults are looking for you. They know about you. They're knocking on your door.

By now you've figured it out: There's a conflict between Christianity and the cults.

The first thing to remember about that clash is this: There's no neutral ground. There's no way for peace to exist between the two sides. Both sides believe—firmly—two facts: 1) Their message is true for *everyone*, and 2) If you don't embrace that message, you are lost—without God, without his presence in your life now, without the expectation of living eternally in his presence in heaven.

No Gumby-like flexy-bendy here. For Christians, our unchangeable, meant-for-the-whole-world message is contained in the Gospel of Jesus Christ: "For God so loved the world that he gave his one and only Son, that whoever believes in him shall not perish but have eternal life" (John 3:16). Cults often use the same language. They may talk about the Gospel, too. They may name themselves after Jesus, but they always change *something* that redefines the central truths of the Gospel message. They think they're right, and they want everyone to believe what they do. We try to evangelize them; they try to convert us.

And the cults are after *you*.

You may not think you have much to fear from the well-rehearsed stiffs at your door. Or the people who wander airports wearing togas. Or that girl or guy who catches your eye.

You might not think you need to know how to defend yourself.

You might not think that if you knew those guys had a spiritual deathray fixed on your forehead.

Sign on the Dotted Line

Many cults aggressively pursue Christian teens and young adults. It's easy to understand why.

You're already interested in God stuff.

You're already willing to sacrifice for your beliefs.

You're already trained to follow spiritual leaders.

All they have to do is get you to sign on the dotted line and turn yourself over to their ultimate authority, and *poofo!* Insta-cultist.

Cults have ways to make your brain itch, to start you

doubting the beliefs your parents and your church have instilled in you. Some of their questions are valid. Any truth-loving person should be able to handle those questions without hesitation. But a lot of their arguments are booby trapped with explosive untruths.

So exactly how do cults persuade people to convert to their side? Their methods are all variations on one theme: What you have isn't good enough—and what we have is better.

Cult Attack Tactic #1: *You can't trust your church.*

Your church has misled you, they say. Then they offer to tell you all sorts of ways your church biffs and bozos.

This approach comes in multiple flavors. Each cultic group presents a different list to get you to question the validity of what you've been taught:

Mormons tell you the Church went apostate—totally lost true faith—and had to be restored by *their* founder.

Jehovah's Witnesses tell you all of Christendom is in apostasy, evidenced by the fact that churches celebrate holidays like Christmas, which they say is "pagan."

Christian Scientists argue the Church has been infected by thinking that leads you away from the *real* truth you can find only in their writings and teachings.

Of course, we do the same thing in reverse. We want Jehovah's Witnesses, for example, to question the credibility of their leaders, the Watchtower Bible and Tract Society. So what's the crucial difference between our tactics and theirs? It should be honesty. If we're to get anywhere, we should focus on truth issues, accurately reporting what the cult group has taught and carefully demonstrating how their own beliefs are inconsistent with the Bible's teachings, with history, or even with their own doctrines.

Cults, however, often employ myths, legends, and out-and-out false information to get you to question your faith. They twist history and tell you that the Trinity was "made up" hundreds of years after Jesus went back to heaven. They snow you with the idea that the Bible has been corrupted and changed over time to fit the ideas of a spiritually dead Church. Most of the time the person trying to convert you isn't even aware that this "information" they share with you is false. They've been deceived by others, and they simply duplicate the deception.

Cult Attack Tactic #2: *You need a better, higher authority than you can get from the Bible.*

Your church, they charge, along with its pastors, elders, and deacons, is grotesquely inadequate. You need an infallible, error-proof authority you can only get from *them.*

This approach is almost universal among the cults. Mormons direct you to their "Prophet" for the final word on what the Bible *really* means, and the Witnesses have a set of leaders—the "Governing Body"—that tells them how to interpret the Bible. Cults inevitably attack what Bible students call "the sufficiency of Scripture." They say the Bible isn't enough to figure out faith. They say that you can't really understand what the Bible teaches and that you need *their* help. Or that someone has corrupted the Bible and only *their* leader(s) can fix it. Or that you need a different translation of the Bible—one produced by *their* scholars, of course—to get it right.

Get the pattern? They assault your ability to read God's

truth in the Bible for yourself. They assert your need for some new authority—other writings, a hierarchy of leaders, or one massive single figure. And they assure you that *they* have the cure to all the spiritual confusion out there. It's a confident, we-have-all-the-answers attitude that wows a lot of people.

Cult Attack Tactic #3: *You need our NEW discovery—an improvement on what Christians have always taught.*

Here's the heart of why cults exist: They each claim to possess a *new truth* no one has ever spotted before, a *whopper insight* that the rest of Christendom somehow missed for two thousand years.

Beware of folks who try to sell you "new" ideas. Sure, there's lots of Christian truth that is new to *you*—that's what spiritual growth is all about. But there's nothing new under the sun. You won't find any new beliefs you need to add to the Bible. In fact, you can't even find any truly fresh false teachings. Everything that seems new is actually a bowlful of reheated, rechewed, regurgitated *old* false teaching.

God serves up something better than grossly moldy Heresy Hotdish. All that God wants you to know is contained in "the faith that was once for all entrusted to the saints" (Jude 1:3). The Gospel needs to be *relearned* by every generation. But it doesn't need to be *reinvented* by every generation. So don't be afraid to stand up and say, "Hey, don't tell us you've come up with something 'new' that no one has seen before. The Gospel is enough for every generation of Christians—if it's not enough for you, you have a real problem."

45

Cult Attack Tactic #4: *You need to join us because we're really cool, neat folks.*

This one gets hard. No one can say that all the cultists are rude, mean people. They *often* do many nice things. It's impossible to ignore the positive parts of their faith.

At school you might feel drawn to kids you'd be sad to call "cultists." They might be the only ones trying to stay out of trouble and stay on task. They might be the only ones left standing at the end of a party. In a lot of ways, they might look just like you. In a few ways, they might even seem better than you. They're into their faith. Enthusiastic. Idealistic. Motivated. Besides that, their churches can hold a dance without the board booting the youth pastor the next day.

Slap this on top of that: Many cult groups produce moral people. They emphasize family. They demonstrate commitment to wives, husbands, and children. They take care of their own folks, feed the needy, and build good educational systems. Their people sacrifice time and money to further their cause.

To non-Christians, all these things make them *good*. Even *Christian*. And compared to the image those folks project, the people you share a pew with at your own church can start to look pretty sickly.

Good-for-Nothing Good Stuff

Ouch. If cultists can be so neat, why criticize them? If we can't beat them, why not join them? After all, isn't God intensely interested in us being good?

Don't defect to the other team just yet, sport.

You can take inspiration from their dedication. Better to get yourself going and growing than to feel guilty.

You can find a Christian church that's jazzed about Jesus. Better to stick close to a group of people really following God than to feel stuck by yourself.

You can be honest about cultists' shortcomings. Better to be discerning than dazzled and duped.

And *you can see things from God's point of view.* That, after all, is the only point of view that really counts.

Good works please God. *Real* good works, that is. The only good works that please him come from the inside out—from a heart that is right with him. The Bible says it bluntly: A person who isn't right with God cannot please him (Romans 8:5–8).

All the good works in the world won't make a cultist a Christian. It seems obvious, but get this: Only Christ makes Christians. When you see people who do good yet deny the truth about Christ or his Gospel, sound an alarm: *Ah-ooooga! Ah-oooo-ga!* Something is wrong! Truth and action go together. One without the other accomplishes nothing. You can be a nice, moral person and still hate the true God.

The moral? Learn a bit of biology: You don't go *bah bah* to *become* a sheep, you go *bah bah* because you *are* one. What? Well, you can dress up in wool and crawl around on all fours and *bah* all you want, but that won't make you a sheep. You have to be a sheep *on the inside* to be a *real* sheep. Then when you go *bah bah*, it comes naturally, from the inside.

Accept No Counterfeits

Even with all the information in *What's With the Dudes at the Door?*—data about how cults twist Christian belief, details of cult tactics, even dire warnings that *you* are a target—you may wonder why we all can't just quit calling one another names and accept one another.

Picture this. Across the street from where you live, there's a neglected house owned by an eccentric old man. One day the old guy totters out of the house and with his cane motions you over to his yard. You've never talked to him. You worry about weirdos. You fear getting swallowed by shoulder-high grass. But you're curious. He seems nice. You go. The man promises you a healthy hunk of money to straighten up his yard. You sweat over the lawn, water the shrubs, even carve a bush to look like Barney—your little way of making the house look less scary. Hours later the man hands you a crisp hundred-dollar bill. You float home, clutching more money than you've ever made in one shot.

Your parents remind you to be responsible. They point you to your bank. You fill out a deposit slip, and the teller takes your hundred smackers.

But then the teller calls for the bank manager. "Where did you get this bill?" she grills. "You need to step over here. I have some questions for you." You look puzzled. She eyes you, estimating your evilness. Her next words go through you like a bullet: "We can't take this bill. It isn't real."

What would you feel? *Ripped off.* What would you be? *Poor.*

Counterfeit currency works fine as long as it stays in your piggy bank. Cash printed in your neighbor's basement may look like the real thing, but try to go spend it. It's worthless. If it's money you need for food to eat, you'll starve. And all the time and effort you expended to get it is gone. Forever.

They Don't Know What They're Missing

You don't want funny faith any more than you want funny money.

Funny money gets you nothing.

Funny faith gets you nowhere.

It's impossible to live and let live. The fake faith of cults rips off the souls of real people. Maybe yours. Certainly the souls of cultists around the world.

So here's why having real faith is really important.

Only when you have the real truth can you have a relationship with the real God.

You've spotted them at school: *hunka hunka* shrines—lockers plastered top to bottom with photos of movie stars or musicians. Watch between classes and you can see girl gazing at her wallpaper guy. She thinks that she has a relationship with her fantasy man. That he *knows* her. That he *cares* about her. The worst is his life-size face-shot mounted next to a mirror—where she sees herself cheek to cheek with her man.

Guys, say it together: *Sick. Sick. Sick.* (Then go ahead and rip down those pictures in *your* lockers.)

Pictures don't love back. You can't have a relationship with a fantasy. Likewise, you can't worship or love an unreal god. The god offered by the cults doesn't exist. A nonexistent god can't answer prayer. Can't change your life. Can't guide you. Without the real God, there's no forgiveness and no heaven. You can't say you love God if you don't care about the real him. If you love him, you want to know the truth about him. In fact, the Bible says Christians are people who

49

believe, know, do, and *love* the truth (1 Timothy 4:3; 1 John 1:6, 2:21; 2 Thessalonians 2:10).

Only when you have a real relationship with God can you have God's peace.

The scariest cults browbeat you and give you a cyanide-punch gargle. The smoothest cults deceive you with sweet-ness—a toothy little bit country, little bit rock 'n' roll. But God has something better for his people.

Cults don't offer the safety of God's protection. The Bible says that when we have been made right with God "we have peace with God through our Lord Jesus Christ" (Roman 5:1). As you live close to him and pray to him about all your needs, "the peace of God, which transcends all understand-ing, will guard your hearts and your minds in Christ Jesus" (Philippians 4:7). Ditch a relationship with the real God, and you ditch that peace.

Cults don't offer the safety of God's people. The teach-ings of the cults bust through boundaries of belief that the Church has recognized for the past two millennia—doc-trines agonized over by the Church for centuries and re-stated by Reformers like Luther and Calvin. Compared to the hot new lines of the cults, what the Church has held to be true about God and Christ might feel like the Dull-mobile—a car you wouldn't pick for a fun run around town. But unlike the new models, the old roadster is road tested. It won't drop its engine on the ground and leave you stranded a million miles from nowhere.

Only when you have real peace will you show God's love.

You might be thinking, *Okay, so their beliefs might be a little strange, but they seem so honest, and from the world's view, some of them have it all together. I'll look like a moron if I say anything about this—especially if I stand up and say that they really aren't what they seem!*

You might need to rethink. God gives you his peace to pass it on.

Our world is a burning building. God didn't intend the truth of his real Good News just to save your skin. He intends it to save the world.

If he's rescued you, then you can pull others from the flames. It's a starting point to stay cult-free yourself. But your end goal is to help set others free from the cults.

Why not just get along? What's at stake?

Everything. At least everything that matters, anyway.

Think About This Stuff:

1. In what ways are people free to choose spiritual error? In what ways are they not?
2. How do cult members view Christian beliefs and churches? What four attacks do cults typically launch?
3. What positive traits are some cultists known for? Are these things true of the cult members you know?
4. If cultists have these positive qualities, why is it important to draw a line between cults and real Christianity? What does it matter if a person's faith is counterfeit?
5. What does true faith offer that the messages of cults can't?

**"Your word is
a lamp to my feet
and a light
for my path."**

—Psalm 119:105

Brush Up on Your Own Beliefs

chapter 4

Midway through the movie *Gettysburg*—the way-best Civil War movie ever made—there's a burst of major drama. Dim candlelight reveals the face of Confederate commander Robert E. Lee. But his eyes blaze fire as he blasts Jeb Stuart, a general serving under him. Why? Lee trusted Stuart to gather information for him about the lay of the land held by his own army and the strength and position of the Union enemy. But Stuart had instead galloped off with the cavalry, leaving Lee's troops fatally exposed.

Put yourself in Lee's boots. You don't know where you are, where your enemy is, or how you're going to defend the position you've taken.

You're flapping in the breeze.

You might as well flee the battlefield.

Christians often imitate the devoted but dense Jeb Stuart. Lots of believers get excited, grab their swords, and run off in any ol' direction looking for a fight—even though they know little about what they are supposed to believe and even less about what others believe. They don't know where the attackers are or what ground they should protect. The results can be as disastrous for the Christian as they proved to be for Lee's army in 1863.

Before you can think about answering the claims of cults, there's something you gotta be sure of:

It's way more important to know the truth than it is to know a lie.

It's tough to defend a faith you don't understand.

It's cocky to worry about someone else's beliefs before you know your own.

It's far more important to know true, biblical Christianity than it is to swallow a book's worth of facts about groups that claim to be Christian but aren't. Besides, if you know the *real thing* real well, you'll easily recognize *counterfeits* when they come along.

You need to learn what cults believe, but you also need to understand *well* what Christianity says about God, Jesus, and the Bible—the three big points that are keys to spotting cultic beliefs. What you really need is a map of the Christian position—the lay of the land, the landmarks that give you a sense of direction, the lines that you must defend. Then you'll see where the cults swarm against you in battle.

Big Point #1: God Is God

You'd better get ready to get decked when your parents ask you about the new love of your life and all you can say is, "Well, she's cute." They'll rampage if all you can blurt is, "He has a nice personality." If you're seriously in love, you'll have a seriously huge memory for tiny details about how he or she looks, acts, talks, and walks.

Nobody with more than half a brain ever bought the line "Hello, I love you, won't you tell me your name?" Love is based on knowledge. It's a problem to say you love God yet not know all you can about him.

You probably know a lot about *what God does*: He made you. Died for you. Lives in you.

You likewise are probably learning *what God is like*: Loving. Just. Faithful.

You may have thought less about *who God is*. God's actions and character don't come from nowhere. Maybe no one has ever taught you what he's about at the core of his being: Eternal. All-powerful. All-knowing. Morally flawless. Unchanging. Triune.

Christians' most basic conviction about God is that he's *one of a kind*. There's only one God, and he's not taking applications for a replacement.

God *is* God.

Always *has been* God.

Always *will be* God.

Period.

"Absolute monotheism" is the technical term, but it simply means an uncompromising belief in *one God*. Christians don't believe in a God who became a god, evolved to be a god, or in any way has ever been less than he is today. We don't believe in other gods, whether they be lesser, dinky deities or competing gods in some distant galaxy. We believe that there is one God, eternal, unchanging, with all power.

But why do you believe that? How do you defend that?

A well-prepared soldier knows where his weapons are and what they do. The *one* way you can get prepped is by mulling and memorizing Scripture. It's the basis of what true Christians believe, and memorizing it isn't as hard as it sounds. Just like lyrics, locker combinations, and phone numbers get permanently lodged in your brain, the Bible can stick there. It's a matter of focus and a bit of time—making it important. Memorizing makes you quick on the draw when you share your faith, able to aim a verse without having to look it up. Having God's Word in your heart (Psalm 119:11) not only helps you better defend your faith, it radically changes your Christian life and draws you closer to God.

So here are just a few good passages that support the belief that *there's one God who has always been God.* Stick some in your head:

Bible Proof: There Is One God Who Has Always Been God

- Deuteronomy 6:4–5, NASB: "Hear, O Israel! The LORD is our God, the LORD is one! You shall love the LORD your God with all your heart and with all your soul and with all your might."
- Psalm 90:2: Before the mountains were born or you brought forth the earth and the world, from everlasting to everlasting you are God.
- Isaiah 43:10: "You are my witnesses," declares the LORD, "and my servant whom I have chosen, so that you may know and believe me and understand that I am he. Before me there was no God formed, and there will be none after me."

Hefting the Theological Furniture

God is One. It'd be easy to grasp who God is if what we knew about him stopped there. But God is also a "Trinity," a union of three persons with one nature—Father, Son, and Holy Spirit.

"Trinity" sounds like a heavy hunk of theological furniture—like a sofa that's easier to drop off a third-floor balcony than it is to carry upstairs. But as hard as it is to lug upward, you don't want to try to live without it. Without the "doctrine of the Trinity," the Christian has no place to rest because it wraps together a whole lot of what we believe about God. It's what God has revealed about himself. And it's one of the lines where cults stare you down from the other side.

There are three big, interrelated truths to remember about the Trinity. Get these down and you'll get the idea:

- God has just one BEING. "Being" is what makes something what it is—rather than something else. Sound strange? Well, you've got a people being, not a cat, dog, or jelly being. There is only one BEING of God, and that's what makes God God.
- That one BEING of God is possessed by three PERSONS—the Father, the Son, and the Holy Spirit. That doesn't mean that the Father *is* the Son or that the Son *is* the Spirit. They're three *persons* and one *being*, three *whos* and one *what*. The *what* of God is his being, the *who* of God is the three persons—Father, Son, and Spirit.
- The Father, Son, and Holy Spirit are therefore EQUAL with one another. The Father isn't "better" than the Son or "more God" than the Son. This third point teaches the "deity of Christ" (Jesus is truly God, not just a man) and the "deity of the Holy Spirit" (the Spirit is truly God,

not just a force or influence).

The Trinity *doesn't* mean that there are three persons who are one person. (Do the math. That would be a contradiction.) It also *doesn't* mean that three beings are one being. (That wouldn't work, either.) Finally, it *doesn't* mean there are three "gods" who are one "God." When we say the Father is God, and the Son is God, and the Spirit is God, we are talking about their *nature*. Each fully and completely possesses the "divine nature."

A hint on getting to know the core of God: To understand the Trinity you have to catch the difference between *being* and *person*. They aren't the same thing. A rock—even a pet rock—has *being* but it doesn't have *person*. You can rag on a rock all day long and it won't care, since it isn't *personal*. But *you* are a being, a human being, who is personal—despite what your brother or sister says. You are you, not somebody else. Your *being* is shared by one person: the one and only you. In God's case, his being isn't limited to time and space like yours and mine. So his being can be shared by *three Persons*: the Father, the Son, and the Spirit.

Father, Son, and Spirit: Totally God

Each member of the Trinity is an absolutely individual identity—and is absolutely God. When it comes to answering cult claims, it's especially crucial to remember the reality of Jesus' divinity. Jesus is God. If he isn't God, then his death couldn't save us. He'd be just a nice guy who finished last. He'd be just one of many brilliant teachers—smart, but not worthy of your life. He'd be crazy—because he claimed to be God. And exactly how important is it that we recognize his full "Godhood"? 1 John 2:23 says this: "No one who denies the Son has the Father; whoever acknowledges the Son has the Father also." Without accepting Jesus for who he is, we don't know God at all.

Munch on this: Even though God has shown himself to us as a Trinity, every cult system fiercely denies some part of the Trinity. Examples: Oneness ("Jesus Only") Pentecostals say that what we see in Jesus is all there is of God—they deny that there are three persons in the Trinity. Jehovah's Witnesses deny that Jesus is fully God—they forget that all three persons share one eternal divine being. And many cults believe the Holy Spirit is a force or a farce—they forget Father, Son, and Spirit are co-equal. (A less-than-adequate understanding of the Trinity, by the way, isn't just a problem for the cults. Being ignorant of the roles and relationship of Father, Son, and Holy Spirit leads to wacky stuff even within the Church.)

Cultists make it a big deal that the word "Trinity" doesn't appear in the Bible. It doesn't need to. The word "paperback" isn't in the Bible, either, but you've got one in your hands. A word doesn't have to appear in the Bible for it to describe something that really exists. Even so, the idea of Trinity *is* in the Bible: It's the sum of several points the Bible clearly teaches. We need to put them together to make sense of what God tells us about himself.

There are three kinds of Bible passages that support Christians' belief in the Trinity. First, there are verses that mention the Father, Son, and Spirit together (the "Trinitarian passages"). Then there are passages that teach the deity of Christ. (Quite a few are listed for the simple reason that this is one of the main areas where the cults attack the

Christian faith.) Finally, there are plenty of passages that teach that the Holy Spirit is more than a fuzzy feeling—and fully God. (Many cults deny the Holy Spirit is personal, let alone truly God.) Think about these:

Bible Proof: The Trinity

- Ephesians 4:4–6, NASB: There is one body and one Spirit, just as also you were called in one hope of your calling; one Lord, one faith, one baptism, one God and Father of all who is over all and through all and in all.
- 2 Corinthians 13:14, NASB: The grace of the Lord Jesus Christ, and the love of God, and the fellowship of the Holy Spirit, be with you all.
- Matthew 28:19, NASB: "Go therefore and make disciples of all the nations, baptizing them in the name of the Father and the Son and the Holy Spirit."

Bible Proof: The Deity of Christ

- John 1:1: In the beginning was the Word, and the Word was with God, and the Word was God.
- John 20:28: Thomas said to him, "My Lord and my God!"
- Titus 2:13, NASB: . . . looking for the blessed hope and the appearing of the glory of our great God and Savior, Christ Jesus.
- 2 Peter 1:1: Simon Peter, a servant and apostle of Jesus Christ, to those who through the righteousness of Christ have received a faith as precious as ours.
- Philippians 2:5–6, NASB: Have this attitude in yourselves which was also in Christ Jesus, who, although He existed

in the form of God, did not regard equality with God a thing to be grasped.

■ Colossians 2:9: For in Christ all the fullness of the Deity lives in bodily form.

Bible Proof: The Holy Spirit

■ Acts 5:3–4, NASB: But Peter said, "Ananias, why has Satan filled your heart to lie to the Holy Spirit and to keep back *some* of the price of the land? While it remained *unsold*, did it not remain your own? And after it was sold, was it not under your control? Why is it that you have conceived this deed in your heart? You have not lied to men but to God." (*Lying to the Holy Spirit is lying to God.*)

■ 1 Corinthians 12:11, NASB: But one and the same Spirit works all these things, distributing to each one individually just as He wills. *(Get the point? Only a personal being can have a will.)*

You might think you wouldn't wrestle a Mormon to the mat for this stuff. Or out-jog a Jehovah's Witness. Or show a member of The Way a better way. Yet when they say, "God is like . . ." and then blabber a falsehood, they're misunderstanding and misrepresenting your Lord. They're putting down your God. And they're leading people astray in an eternal kind of way. If you know your stuff, you can respectfully respond, "No, the Bible says God is really like *this*." Remember: As tough as it may be to grasp at first, Trinity and divinity is basic Bible information about who God is. If God got a driver's license, this is what would be etched on it in gold letters.

Big Point #2: What Jesus Did

You probably know the basics of the Gospel, a word that literally means "Good News." The Good News is that God takes people who are his enemies and makes them his friends. Before God grabs hold of us, we're alienated from him. Before we come to know Jesus, our relationship with God is dead. We're soaked in sin and can't save ourselves from his righteous anger. But get this Good News: God does for us what we can't do for ourselves. God didn't just provide a way for us to be close to him again—Jesus *became* the way through his death for us (Hebrews 10:20–23). He doesn't tell us to fix ourselves—he saves us by his power (Romans 5:6). He doesn't charge admission to his Kingdom—he plucks us from spiritual death and freely gives us new life (Romans 6:23).

But *how*? How does God turn sinners into his kids? How does he manage to make sworn enemies love him? How can a flawlessly holy God have dealings with people who are so messed up?

He does it in one way and one way only: Jesus. By his death on the cross, Jesus took the punishment we deserve as sinners—death (Romans 3:23). It's incredible. He bears the punishment of those who believe in him. He takes our sin and gives us his perfect life. He takes our guilt and helplessness and gives us forgiveness and power to live his way. What a deal! That's the Gospel true Christians believe—the Good News of Jesus Christ.

Really Good News

The goal of God's Good News is *peace*.

He declares you not guilty—okay with him. What the Bible calls "justified."

When you're justified, you can stand before God without worrying that he's going to zap you for your sins. Why? Because your sins have been taken care of by Christ. He took your punishment, so now you have peace with God (Romans 5:1). You can have a relationship with God where you aren't walloped by fear of punishment—but filled with love and thankfulness for all he's done for you.

Christians are people who know God's peace. Christians are people who've said, "Yes, God. I believe in you. I trust that Christ died on my behalf. I don't have to prove myself to you. Thanks for forgiving me. I want to follow you." They've received the gift God gives in the Gospel.

Problem is, cults are party poopers. They try to hand the gift back to God. God's Good News mutates into the cults' Bad News when you forget two key words: *grace* and *faith*.

God's actions toward you flow completely from *grace*—from favor you haven't earned. You can't add to it, take away from it, or work for it. You don't need to. But cults try. They radically mess with God's plan for knowing him. Being good to win God's favor or seeing grace as a boost that gets you going so you can make it the rest of the way on your own power—those approaches toss out God's way of relating to him. They forget the fact that from start to finish, being accepted and perfected by God comes from God's grace. "By grace you have been saved, through faith" is how Paul put it (Ephesians 2:8).

That *faith* is how you think and act in response to God's grace. Faith doesn't whine. It doesn't come to God and try to strike a deal. *When you have faith, you accept what God says about you.* You don't try to earn something from God. You don't say, "Hey, God, look at all the neat things I've done—witnessing, doing a mission, being moral." Faith is the complete opposite of bloated bigheadedness. It's honest. It doesn't try to bluff God. *When you have faith, you accept God's way of having friendship with him.* You realize you're lost—you can't know God apart from Christ. But with Jesus you're in his family.

Make sure you're holding on to him *alone.* By grace. Through faith. Because Jesus won't play second fiddle. It's not Jesus *plus,* it's Jesus *alone.* Any other supposedly "Good News" is really big-time Bad News. And if you buy the Bad News, you're still God's enemy.

Here's the Good News straight from God's Word:

Bible Proof: Jesus Saves

- John 5:24, NASB: "Truly, truly, I say to you, he who hears My word, and believes Him who sent Me, has eternal life, and does not come into judgment, but has passed out of death into life."
- Romans 3:28: For we maintain that a man is justified by faith apart from observing the Law.
- Romans 4:4–5: Now when a man works, his wages are not credited to him as a gift, but as an obligation. To the man who does not work but trusts in God who justifies the wicked, his faith is credited as righteousness.
- Romans 5:1, NASB: Therefore having been justified by faith, we have peace with God through our Lord Jesus Christ.
- Ephesians 2:8–10, NASB: For by grace you have been saved through faith; and that not of yourselves, *it is* the gift of God; not as a result of works, so that no one may

boast. For we are His workmanship, created in Christ Jesus for good works, which God prepared beforehand, that we should walk in them.

■ Titus 3:5–7: He saved us, not because of righteous things we had done, but because of his mercy. He saved us through the washing of rebirth and renewal by the Holy Spirit, whom he poured out upon us generously through Jesus Christ our Savior, so that having been justified by his grace, we might become heirs having the hope of eternal life.

Big Point #3: The Bible Is Enough

So how do you know for sure that there's one true God, that the Trinity is for real, and that the Gospel is a message of grace we grasp by faith? Because you have a sure word from God, a revelation of his truth that's firm and unchanging.

God's Word—the Bible—describes itself as "God-breathed" (2 Timothy 3:16—many translations read "inspired"). What does that mean? To be "God-breathed" means to come straight from God's mouth. The breath of God is about as personal as you can get. Breath forms words. Breath is life. So Scripture is God talking straight to human beings. Jesus told the Jews that when they read Scripture they were hearing *God speaking to them* (Matthew 22:31).

What's more, the faith revealed in the Bible needs no additions. No new books. No total reinterpretations. It's complete and clear. Jude wrote and urged his readers to "contend for the faith that was *once for all* entrusted to the saints" (Jude 1:3, italics added).

Every cult finds a way to ditch the Bible's ultimate authority—the Bible's status as the final test of all teaching and of Christian truth. There are zillions of ways to do it. You can

- *Add your own Scripture.* A real favorite, and easy to do, too!
- *Edit the Bible you already have.* Don't like a particular Bible passage? Delete it! Or—if you're truly crafty—just mistranslate it! That's the tricky way. After all, how many Greek scholars are going to double-check your work?
- *Make yourself indispensable.* The all-time cult favorite is "You can't understand the Bible without *our* help!" That way, they can let you have the Bible but tell you it's a closed book without their interpretations, understandings, or traditions.

When anyone comes along and says, "Hey, the Scriptures aren't enough. You need _____," be on guard. Jesus and the apostles taught that the Bible was God speaking, and they didn't tell us to look to anything else. Follow their lead.

Bible Proof: What the Bible Says About Itself

- 2 Timothy 3:16–17: All Scripture is God-breathed and is useful for teaching, rebuking, correcting and training in righteousness, so that the man of God may be thoroughly equipped for every good work.
- 2 Peter 1:20–21: Above all, you must understand that no prophecy of Scripture came about by the prophet's own

interpretation. For prophecy never had its origin in the will of man, but men spoke from God as they were carried along by the Holy Spirit.

- John 17:17: Your word is truth.
- Psalms 119:151–152: Yet you are near, O LORD, and all your commands are true. Long ago I learned from your statutes that you established them to last forever.

Sit on It For Sure

Cults abuse and misuse Bible teachings besides who God is, what Jesus has done, and what we use as the source of our beliefs. But those are the biggies that form the basics of Christian faith. Missing these truths means missing God.

You know better. You know the truths that tell you about God.

You can rely on these truths. Rest in them—even if at first they seem hard to hoist.

Look at it like this: If you claim you *believe* a couch will hold you up, how do you prove it? You don't sit down dainty—hanging on to a wall or a chair, or lowered in by a winch. You throw your bod at it. You take a running start and swine dive into the sweet spot. You don't worry the couch will collapse and send you sprawling.

That's how real faith works. If the thing you put your faith in fails, you're in big trouble. Thankfully, Jesus Christ *never* fails. You can plop yourself—and your eternal future—on him.

Think About This Stuff:

1. How are Christians like the devoted but dense Jeb Stuart?

2. What does it mean that Christians believe in *one* God? What biblical proof do you have for this belief?

3. Think hard: Describe how God can be a Trinity—one being and three persons? Why do true Christians believe this?

4. How do you know that Jesus and the Holy Spirit are God?

5. What did Jesus accomplish for Christians? What does it mean that "Jesus saves"?

6. Why do you rely on the Bible as your sole, sufficient source of your Christian beliefs?

"I am the LORD,
and there is
no other;
apart from me
there is no God."

—*Isaiah 45:5*

Space Gods From Kolob

chapter 5

You're on a *looooong* bus ride, a field trip to someplace a million miles away. A bunch of your friends know you're a Christian—the *real* kind, committed, serious, and willing to share your faith with others. Well, there's a new kid in class. He seems cool enough. Cuss-free. Sorta clean-cut. Moral. Smart. Good friend material.

Right after the bus starts rumbling down the road, a friend pops a question about the Bible. You respond. The new kid scoots closer to listen in. The conversation goes on, and then he jumps in.

"That's interesting. I've read the Bible a lot, too. But God has more to say than just what's in the Bible."

"More?" you ask. "What do you mean?"

"Well, think about it. God loves people in the Americas as much as he loves people over in Israel. Don't you think if he loves them, he'd give his word to them, too?"

You've never heard anything like this before. You're zigging. He's zagging. You need details. "What do you think he would need to add to the Bible?"

"I believe God gave his word to the ancient inhabitants of the Americas and that we have that revelation in the *Book of Mormon*."

OH NO! He's a MORMON! Your brain strains to pull up everything you've ever heard about Mormons, but nothing coherent comes to mind. Everyone looks at you, expecting deep words of wisdom. "Oh, really?" is all you manage. Then it hits you. "Say, don't Mormons believe God was once a man—or something like that?" *Whew*. Quick save! A few of the people sitting around you gasp. Others think you jest.

"Yes, actually, the Church of Jesus Christ of Latter-day Saints does teach that God is an exalted man, just as the Bible indicates."

Zzzaaappp. You start to sweat. You didn't expect that. The Bible teaches that God is an exalted man? You're in way over your head now. How far till we get to that crazy place, anyway? "The Bible teaches that?" you hear someone say in a faint, unfamiliar voice. *Yikes*. That was you! Why on earth did you say that?

"Sure," he replies. He seems so confident. You're about to get planted six feet deep. You don't even have your Bible! Why didn't you try harder in that last Bible drill? You wish your verse memorization list was a *lot* longer just about now. But who'da ever thunk you'd talk to somebody who thinks God is an overgrown man!? "Sure it does. The Bible often speaks of God's hands, eyes, feet, and so on."

"But those are just figurative." Heads turn back to him. It's Bible Ping-Pong.

"I'd rather take the Bible literally, actually," he says. "Besides, the Bible says that there are 'Gods many and lords many' in 1 Corinthians 8:5, and the Lord Jesus spoke of 'gods' in John 10:34." He knew those references off the top of his head! He doesn't even have a Bible or whatever it is they use!

"So you believe that God was once a man? Don't you also believe that we can become gods, too?"

"Yes, that's true. One of our prophets put it this way: 'As man is, God once was; as God is, man may become.' It's a glorious promise that we can become like our heavenly Father. Just as Jesus said in Matthew 5:48, 'Be perfect, therefore, as your heavenly Father is perfect.' "

"But that doesn't make us gods, or God an exalted man," you manage to reply. Then from out of nowhere a verse comes to mind, and you're shocked to hear it spill from your mouth: "The Bible says that there is only one true God, and that he's always been God. Psalm 90:2 says, 'Before the mountains were born or you brought forth the earth and the world, from everlasting to everlasting you are God.' " In a flash you remember a Sunday school teacher *years ago* teaching you that passage.

Bus Rides and Big Bible Questions

How well would you do on that kind of Bible-intensive bus ride? Would you be in the driver's seat? Or would you get shoveled out the rear exit?

Sadly, a Christian often reacts in one of two ways: 1) He or she ridicules the person rather than responding with God's truth. It's what happens if you don't know your own faith thoroughly enough to answer challenges presented to you. Hot arguments happen when you don't know your own view well enough to discuss it calmly. 2) The Christian is rattled—maybe even convinced—by the views expressed and starts down the road to conversion to another faith. In either case, one thing is for sure: The person involved in a cult rarely stumbles across a well-prepared Christian who can provide a "reason for the hope" she or he has in Christ (1 Peter 3:15).

The Mormon guy on the bus wasn't a fluke. Each year thousands of well-prepared young LDSers head off on missions for their church, spending two years proclaiming the gospel according to Mormonism. Because the Mormons aggressively send out these missionaries—and because the Mormon church is growing rapidly—they're the cultists you're most likely to run into.

The LDS Church holds tight to the claim to be Christian yet denies the most basic Christian teachings. The world sees Mormons as just another group of conservative, even fundamentalist, Christians. Yet by looking at their beliefs, how they present them, and how they defend them, we see how cults grow—especially how they convert people to their point of view. As we check how cults look at the big points of Christian belief—God (this chapter), Jesus (chapter 6), and the Bible (chapter 7)—they'll be our prime example.

The Gods Must Be Crazy

Every cult offers the wrong answers in those three big areas. All three points are crucial. But the single most important test of any religious group is this no-brainer: Who is God? If they miss the right answer on #1, don't bother with the rest of the test. That's the issue that *defines* what it is to be a cult—they claim to be Christian but present a different god. Insta-cult formula.

Strangely, when it comes to Mormonism, what they say about God is the teaching we usually ignore. To Christians, the fact that Mormons believe in many gods is way past weird. And so we don't know how to respond to them. Honestly—how many Bible passages have you memorized that teach there's only one God? That makes it tough to talk.

The Mormon doctrine of God is especially hard for Christians to get because we interpret what they say in our own terms. It's like a wall of language between Christians and Mormons. We use the same terms but mean different things, like we've got the same words but different dictionaries to define our meanings. We try to talk to each other—but what a mess! It's pretty much what happens when Christians and Mormons, majorly dumb about what the other believes, get together to talk God.

So what exactly do Mormons believe about God? That's a topic to fill a book. But here is a short, accurate taste of what Mormons teach. No foolin'.

1. Mormons say they worship only one God. What they mean, though, is that they worship a god who is one *in purpose*. They confess that in fact there are three gods—the Father, the Son, and the Holy Ghost (Mormons prefer to use "Ghost," the term used in the King James Version of the Bible). The Father is one god. The Son is another god, actually begotten by the first god—the Father. And the Holy Ghost is a third god. These gods are united in purpose but are three separate beings. The Father, Son, and Spirit may be rooting for the same team, but they aren't the same being.

2. God was once a man. A couple famous Mormon sayings sum this up. Take two of these and you'll need to call your pastor in the morning:

"As man is, God once was; as God is, man may become."—Mormon Prophet Lorenzo Snow

"God himself was once as we are now, and is an exalted man, and sits enthroned in yonder heavens!" —Mormon Founder Joseph Smith

Take these statements just as they are: God the Father— Mormons call him *Elohim*—was once a man just like any other human guy. He lived on another planet. After his death on that planet, he was exalted to the status of a god. Mormon founder Joseph Smith put it this way:

It is the first principle of the Gospel to know for a certainty the Character of God, and to know that we may converse with him as one man converses with another, and that he was once a man like us; yea, that God himself, the Father of us all, dwelt on an earth, the same as Jesus Christ himself did. . . .

Some Mormons think God the Father was, like Jesus, a Savior of his own planet. He therefore wouldn't have been a sinner. Others say they don't know. Either way, their astounding belief is that God was once a man and only later in time became a god. Again, they aren't teaching that God became a man—like Jesus came "in the flesh"—but that God was once a slob like the rest of us.

3. **God hasn't always been God.** If God was once a man, that means that there was a time—some Mormons say in some "other eternity"—when God wasn't a god. Joseph

Smith said this: "We have imagined and supposed that God was God from all eternity. I will refute that idea, and take away the veil, so that you may see."

If you believe God has always been God (Psalm 90:2), you're wrong—according to Joseph Smith, that is.

4. God isn't the one-and-only God. Tune in here and track this: If God was once a man, he would have needed a god to create the world he lived on as a man. So there's a "god" that existed before "our God." And what was *that* "god" before he became a "god"? Well, a man. So he must have had a god before him, and so on and so forth—back into eternity. That means that there are literally billions of gods in existence *somewhere*. Some Mormons say there are an infinite number of gods. Others don't go that far. In either case, the god of this planet, the Father, is by no means the first God *ever*. Nor will he be the last.

The Mormon Church has gone so far as to tell us a bit about where God lives. According to one of their books of Scripture (the *Book of Abraham*), the planet where God dwells circles a star named "Kolob." Yeah, Kolob. Guess that means you can send God a Christmas card if you want. You've got his address!

5. Mormons believe they themselves can someday become gods. You read that right. Add up all of the above and it means that the righteous Mormon man—if he remains faithful to the church to the end of his life—can upon his death and resurrection receive what the Mormons call "exaltation" and become a "god" worthy of worship. A bit more on that in the next chapter. It's a wild belief way out in the cosmos.

6. There are many gods. The final result of all of this is a belief in what Mormons call "the plurality of gods." A more accurate way of putting it: Mormonism is polytheistic. A polytheist believes in the existence of more than one true God. Christians are monotheists. Mormons are polytheists. If Christianity were golf, Mormons just bagged one into the woods. They aren't even on the fairway. They clearly aren't Christians.

Salesguys for Other Gods

Get the difference? The disagreements between Christianity and Mormonism aren't hard to spot if you know where to look. Cults normally misunderstand exactly how Jesus saves us. And if they goof their use of the Bible, they usually mess the majors of Christian belief. But what makes a cult a cult is that they totally miss the mark on what they believe about God. It couldn't be clearer:

Christianity teaches . . .	Mormonism teaches . . .
There is only one God.	There are many gods.
There are three persons in the Trinity.	There are three gods in the Trinity.
God has always been God.	God was once a man.
Humans can become God's children.	Humans can become gods.

Mormonism isn't the only belief system that biffs biblical Christianity's teachings about God. Grab a glance at a couple other counterfeits.

Jehovah's Witnesses

The Watchtower Bible and Tract Society (Jehovah's Witnesses) pounce on historical Christian teachings on the

Trinity. They're especially fond of attacking Christ's deity and the idea that the Holy Spirit is a Person—rather than just an "it." They pump out scads of books and pamphlets to teach their followers and unsuspecting readers.

Here are quick details on what the Witnesses believe about God:

1. **There is only one God, Jehovah.** Jehovah is sort of a butchered pronunciation of one of God's key Old Testament names. It's better pronounced "Yahweh." Your Bible normally doesn't use that specific name, even when it's in the text. Instead, it shows you that the word is Yahweh by spelling the o-r-d of Lord with small capital letters, like this: LORD.

2. **The first thing Jehovah created was a mighty angel called Michael.** Through Michael, Jehovah created all *other* things. Michael, though, is still a creation, like everything else—not fully God, who doesn't need someone else to zap him into existence.

3. **Jesus is basically Michael the Archangel.** In other words, Jesus isn't God. And today, in fact, there isn't any "Jesus." If you went to heaven you'd see Michael.

4. **The Holy Spirit is "an impersonal active force."** The Holy Spirit—they write it "holy spirit" in their literature—is like electricity or running water. Powerful, but no personality.

All this adds up to

5. **The Witnesses don't believe in the Trinity.** When the Bible talks about being baptized "in the name of the Father and of the Son and of the Holy Spirit" (Matthew 28:19), that's like saying—according to the Witnesses—"in the

name of Jehovah, Michael the Archangel, and an impersonal, active force."

The Bible has a completely different take on things. Jesus—and the Spirit—is just as much God as is the Father. In some Bible passages Jesus and the Spirit look like they're "less" than the Father—passages the cults latch onto to say Jesus is less than the Father. But keep this in mind: The Father, the Son, and the Spirit take *different jobs* in saving people. It wasn't the Father who came to earth to be born in Bethlehem; it was the Son. The Son did something *different* from the Father, but that doesn't make him *less than* the Father—only *different*. Think about it: Since the Son came to earth as a man, he voluntarily submitted himself to the Father (you wouldn't expect the perfect Savior to be an atheist, would you?). And that submission meant obedience and even worship. But that doesn't change the fact that in eternity past, the Son was fully God, co-equal with the Father. In the same way, though the Spirit has taken the role of Comforter—the one who comes into the lives of believers to empower them and change them to look like Christ— that only makes him *different* from the Father and Son, not *less than* them.

The problem? What Jehovah's Witnesses teach is heresy, a whopper falsehood, a violation of a central truth of Christianity. Thing is, it's nothing new. It's a teaching the church condemned in the 4th century—nearly 1,700 years ago!

"Jesus Only" ("Oneness") Pentecostals

All cults mess up on who God is. Remember? It's the key to defining a cult.

One more example.

People called "Jesus Only" or "Oneness" Pentecostals deny the Trinity by saying that Jesus *is* the Father. (Don't confuse this group with other types of Pentecostals—a huge chunk of true Christians who emphasize the work of the Holy Spirit today.) "Jesus Only" adherents say the Trinity isn't real. God, they say, is just one Person. Sometimes God acts like the Father, sometimes like the Son, and sometimes like the Spirit. One way to recognize the cult is by their claim that to be a Christian you must be baptized not in the name of the Father, Son, and Holy Spirit, but in the name of Jesus *only*.

A lot of Christians end up thinking like this group without even knowing it. Yet the Bible is clear in teaching that the Father *sent* the Son (John 8:26) and the Father and Son *send* the Spirit (John 14:26, 16:7). Trying to read the Bible through "Jesus Only" glasses can become ridiculous. A passage like Matthew 3:16–17, for example, makes God look like a gargantuan ventriloquist!

Things to Watch Out For

Whatever cult you look at, there are similarities in how they look at God.

The god cults serve isn't the God of the Bible. Sounds simple. It is. Yet nowadays lots of people run around saying, "Hey, your God, my God—all the same thing!" God isn't into the call-him-by-any-name game. He wiped out entire nations in the Bible for trying that trick. No, he wants people to *know* him, and you can't do that without knowing the *truth* about him.

Cults ditch the total deity of Christ. One big reason it's important to believe in the deity of Jesus is that it took a truly *divine Savior* to redeem you. Michael the Archangel couldn't atone for your sins. You don't want to trust your eternal soul into the hands of a mere *creature*—only Christ in all his divine perfection could pay for your sins. No divine Savior, no divine sacrifice. No divine sacrifice, no divine salvation. Period.

So the cults are always out to make Jesus somebody he isn't. But the Bible warns us about that (2 Corinthians 11:4).

Cults elevate people to God's place. Back when Paul wrote to the Romans, he said that people try to tip God off of his throne, grab a honkin' ladder, and climb up there themselves (Romans 1:18–24). As dumb as the idea is, people try to do it all the time: Get rid of the real God and replace him with something else.

Hanging On to the Real God

It might not be as obvious to you when cults swap in a substitute for the one true God. But when you know what the Bible says about who God is, you can see through the switcheroo. And when you look at what the cults actually teach, the trick is doubly clear.

Now watch what the cults do to Jesus.

Think About This Stuff:

1. How would you react if you were cornered on a bus ride by a cultist? Do you feel prepared?

2. What main points define what Mormonism teaches about God?
3. Contrast what Christianity teaches about God with what Mormonism teaches (hint: check out the chart).
4. What do Jehovah's Witnesses say about God? What do "Jesus Only" Pentecostals teach?
5. What false things should you watch for in how cults talk about God?

**"I am proud
of the Good News,
because it is
the power God uses
to save everyone
who believes."**

—Romans 1:16a, NCV

A Planet to Call Your Own

chapter 6

Drift back to second grade. As your teacher hands you a brochure for the all-school fund-raiser, your eyes widen.

"All you have to do," goozes Mrs. Patuski, "is *sell*. SELL-SELL-SELL!" Christmas wrapping paper. Nuts. Cheese. The school gets money for its new iguana mascot, you get prizes. It's a win-win situation. Your brain whizzes with expectations of easily selling enough to win posters. Skates. Your own VCR. X-ray glasses. A bedroom brimming with lava lamps and black lights. But your eyes glue to a full-color picture of the ultimo prize: a battery-powered radio/light/horn for your bike. You gonna git yourself all of it.

You hit up your relatives. Knock door-to-door through the neighborhood. Trudge far and wide searching out people to buy what you're selling.

On the last day of the fund-raiser you bring your orders and moolah envelope to school.

Your $11 doesn't win much.

A few stickers—a loser prize everyone gets.

Not exactly what you'd planned on.

Paul wrote this: "Do you not know that in a race all the runners run, but only one gets the prize? Run in such a way as to get the prize" (1 Corinthians 9:24). The world is full of people who think they're running toward God. But they're in for a rude surprise. They aren't going to win the prize.

You don't want to join their pack for a jog around the track. You'll die of disappointment when the prize you work for isn't real. You'll expire from exhaustion when the path to the prize isn't clear. True Christianity defines the real treasure at the end of the track. It spells out the clear rules to win.

Unwrapping the Prize

Ever sat around and thought hard about eternity?

Your eyes go glassy.

Your head spins.

Fact is, *finite* minds can't wrap themselves around *infinite* time. You can't grasp what eternity is all about—though those clock-watching last ten minutes of school are surely an *ugly* taste of how long it will last. It's forever. And ever.

So . . . what do you want to be doing for eternity? Ever thought about *that*? Ever mulled your outrageously LONG-TERM goals?

Trick questions. Sunning on the beach or blasting your way to the zillionth level on your favorite video game might somehow figure in, but God already has eternity planned. And his party can be summed up in one person: Jesus Christ. Where you are, who you become, and what you do—they all depend on Jesus. Jesus is at the center of God's plan to save the human race.

Knowing him is the prize—the outcome of your faith.

Knowing him is also the sole path to God—the real way to win.

The Bible calls what Jesus did on the cross "the power of God for salvation" (Romans 1:16). God's Good News is the power of forgiveness. It's the power God uses to melt a heart from one that hates him to one that loves him. It's the power that makes a Christian want to be like him and serve him. That's an even higher-voltage power display than when God heals—makes the sick well, makes the blind see, or even—get this—when God makes the dead rise again.

Sabotaging God's Power Plant

In war there's no quicker way to undo an enemy than to unplug his power supply. Any *Hogan's Heroes* fan can tell you that even Hitler will eventually fall if you clip his high wires, sabotage his generating plants, and blast his power networks.

If the Gospel is God's power to save us, it's no wonder cults attack that point more than any other part of God's truth. They spin the Gospel every way imaginable to ditch the message of salvation by God's grace through faith in Jesus Christ—misdirecting, twisting, distorting, in every possible way confusing the real message of the Gospel of Christ.

Let's look again at Mormonism for an example of how cults fall short of biblical teaching—how they replace the life-giving message of Christ with a message that *sounds* nice but *can't save you.*

Promoted to Godhood

It's a tempting offer: *Be your own God. Rule and reign over planets, solar systems, even galaxies! Have billions of spirit children with multiple wives.* It sounds like *Battlestar Galactica.* Or a *Star Trek* episode when *Q* shows up. Or a fund-raiser that promises you fantabulous prizes for selling cheese logs. Hard as it might be to believe, it's Mormon doctrine.

In the last chapter we saw how God—according to Mormon teaching—was once upon a time a man who lived on another planet. He was exalted to the status of a god. Now, here's the back end of the Mormon equation: "As man is, God once was; *as God is, man may become.*" Wanting to be *godly* is the wish of every Christian. But dreaming of being *a god*? That's what the Mormon hopes for.

A wise Christian once said that "The Gospel isn't that men can become gods, but that God became a man in Jesus Christ." Mormon thinking flips the process on its head. In Mormon belief the goal of God's truth is to exalt sinners— fallen humans—*us*—to the status of God! That's what happened with the god of this planet, and that's the promise held out to worthy Mormon men: Go through the Temple, get sealed to your wife for time and eternity, and eventually someday you'll be a god and start the process all over again.

It sounds wacko that someone would even propose that that's the goal behind God's Good News, because nowhere does the Bible even begin to picture heaven or Christ's work on our behalf in those terms. But it's what Mormon leaders have taught since the beginning. Even people who convert to the LDS Church might be pretty clueless about this doctrine, but it's LDS belief nonetheless.

God's Up in the Nosebleeds

Mormonism rewrites Scripture's teachings. Actually, it's more than a rewrite. Mormonism chucks the Bible's salvation story and sneaks in a new script. The big deal about God saving us—according to the Bible—is that it brings glory, honor, and praise to the Father, Son, and Holy Spirit (Ephesians 1:6). It highlights God's grace. God's mercy. God's purpose. It produces a people eager to serve God and each other, people whose brains and hearts overflow with praise for God (1 Peter 2:9–10).

Christian salvation remembers that God alone rules the universe. Believers are privileged heirs of his grace. Cultic salvation puts people center stage and sends God hiking to the cheap seats. Whenever humans are the primary winners in salvation—slobs promoted to godhood, for example—everything else in the Gospel is messed up and redefined. Let's look at just some of the results:

1. Mormonism teaches two kinds of salvation. "Salvation" ends up having two distinct meanings. First, there is a "general salvation" that applies to everyone—another way of saying "resurrection." That is, in Mormonism everyone will be saved since everyone will be resurrected. Mormons can *say*, "Sure, we believe in salvation by grace," but what they *mean* is they believe that everyone will be *resurrected* by grace. The second kind of "salvation" is exaltation to godhood. Exaltation isn't a gift given with no strings attached. It's acquired by temple endowments and other religious observances and activities. You've got to be *worthy* of exaltation. It's something you *work for*.

You've got to be aware of this difference in terms—salvation and exaltation—and that the same terms have completely different meanings. Loads of conversations between Christians and Mormons go nowhere because neither side understands the distinctions.

2. **People can someday become gods.** The righteous Mormon man who experiences exaltation will take his wife—or wives, depending—and organize matter into another planet. They'll beget spirit children, place them in physical bodies, and start the planetary manufacturing process all over again. Except this time the man gets to be "God" and be worshipped by his children. (Sorry, gals. Women need not apply for membership in this Future Gods of the Universe club. You can only become goddesses under the authority of your husband. And only if you're "sealed" in the Mormon Temple. That means you have to be married to your husband "for time and eternity" in the LDS Temple if you are going to get to become a "goddess." And be prepared: Your husband can be sealed to more than one woman!)

3. **Disobeying God isn't always sin.** Imagine how fuddled your brain would feel if you had to wonder if obeying God's clear commands was really the right thing to do. Or if you thought you had to experience sin to know what good is.

Here's where Mormonism makes sin confusing. Remember Adam and Eve in the Garden of Eden? In Mormon theology, Adam didn't sin when he ate the apple. He transgressed. The difference? God put Adam in a position where he *had* to sin. In fact, since Mormons believe humans all exist as spirit children before coming to this world, God actually chose Adam before he became a man for the special mission of getting things started. And Adam knew he would have to sin.

You see, once Eve ate the apple, she became mortal. That put Adam smack between two conflicting commands from God. First, God told Adam to be "fruitful and multiply," to have kids. Second, God told Adam not to eat the fruit on the tree of the knowledge of good and evil. Adam realized that the only way he could fulfill the first command was to break the second. So he did. The *Book of Mormon* puts it this way:

> And now, behold, if Adam had not transgressed he would not have fallen, but he would have remained in the garden of Eden. . . . And they would have had no children; wherefore they would have remained in a state of innocence, having no joy, for they knew no misery; doing no good, for they knew no sin. . . . Adam fell that men might be; and men are, that they might have joy. (2 Nephi 2:23, 25)

So Adam made the "right" decision. Bit the fruit. Sure, technically he transgressed God's law. But in falling and becoming mortal he fulfilled God's purpose. He planted the human race on this planet.

It's pretty obvious that the Mormon view of sin is radically different from the Bible's view. You don't want to press the logic of "knowing sin to have joy." Any hormone-hopped teenage brain will run toward "Get drunk so you know it's good to be sober." "Get sexed so you know what purity is." "Bash your head against a wall so you'll know how good it feels when it stops." That isn't the way God works. But it's the logical end of Mormon theology. And by the way, did you catch the gargantuan error in the *Book of Mormon*? If one must know sin to do good, what about Jesus, who "knew no sin" (1 Peter 2:22)?

4. **Grace builds on human effort.** How a Mormon gains God's approval is utterly different from God's message of grace. Mormons practice baptism by immersion. They talk about having faith, repenting, believing, etc. But all of these terms have different meanings when they're jerked from their biblical contexts and redefined. For example, think about this passage from the *Book of Mormon*:

> Yea, come unto Christ, and be perfected in him, and deny yourselves of all ungodliness; and if ye shall deny yourselves of all ungodliness, and love God with all your might, mind and strength, then is his grace sufficient for you, that by his grace ye may be perfect in Christ. (Moroni 10:32)

One tiny term in that verse should scream at you: THEN. "*Then* is his grace sufficient for you." You do all these things and *then* Christ's grace will kick in. You pump in as much gas as you've got and *then* God will top off the tank.

That's not grace! Grace is complete. God's approval is total. It can't be bought, purchased, earned, or merited. You can't suck up to God. You can't impress him. You can't buy his love. If you've got to give something to get it, it isn't *grace*.

And look at what you have to do before grace becomes sufficient. *Hmm* . . . deny yourself *all* ungodliness. No sweat, right? Love God with all your might, mind, and strength.

Yep, you meet folks every day able to pull that off, don't you?

Hardly. Being human means messing up. You love yourself or things around you more than you love God. Every time you put yourself or your desires above God, you end up sinning. If you loved him supremely in all things, you wouldn't do that. If you need to rid yourself of every ungodly habit AND love God perfectly *before* grace kicks in, you're in deep trouble. So is every other human being. That's why Christians believe grace is *unmerited favor*. Because of Christ's death, God accepts you the way you are. He wants to grow you, but he starts with you where you're at.

5. Mormonism offers a chance to get right with God after death. Mormons believe that to be acceptable to God you *must* be baptized. Were you to die before you were dunked, another person could be immersed on your behalf. This "baptism for the dead" frees you—the deceased dude—from "spirit prison" and allows you to enter glory. Some Mormons call their participation in temple rituals for those who've died "redeeming the dead."

Everybody Does It

There are a lot of other problems with the Mormon view of salvation, but if you elevate people to a place they don't belong and lower God from the place he does, you can see how the whole system gets out of whack.

Christianity teaches . . .	Mormonism teaches . . .
God saves.	Humans save themselves.
After death, believers spend eternity in heaven.	After death, worthy Mormons populate their own planets.

Salvation leads to godliness. God alone is worthy of worship.	Exaltation leads to godhood. People become objects of worship.

While Mormonism spins the Gospel in unique ways, you can see the same basic thrust all across the spectrum of the cults. They deny what makes the Christian faith unique: 1) God saves, because 2) humans need saving. Cults take away from the glory of God—who alone deserves honor and praise for salvation—and give at least *some* of it to people. Rarely do cults try to take *all* the honor from God and give it to human beings, but neither do they ever give God *all* the credit. People always manage to grab at least *some* credit for helping God out by getting themselves saved.

Flying on Standby

Jehovah's Witnesses, for example, divide salvation up among two different groups. The "elite" group is the "anointed class" of 144,000 individuals. These folks fly first class on the salvation plane. No honey-roasted peanuts and half a can of Coke for these hotshots. They get the full deal, the usual heavenly perks you'd expect for God's chosen.

But since there are so many millions of Jehovah's Witnesses, there's a "great crowd" crammed into the coach section. They don't get the full benefits of Christ's work, they can't directly fellowship with Christ—as in they can't pray to him—and they won't live in heaven. In fact, they don't even have firm reservations to live in a paradise on earth at the end of time. And even if they make it to this lower paradise, the length of their stay is up for grabs. If evil is ever found in eternity, their world will quickly be destroyed. In other words, they have no promise whatsoever of really "making it."

Jehovah's Witnesses live day-in, day-out in this spiritual insecurity. So when the Witnesses observe what Christians would call the Lord's Supper—they do this once a year—in most gatherings no one even partakes of the Supper, since the vast majority of Witnesses don't claim to belong to the anointed class. And those of the great crowd can't partake.

It's truly a budget-class salvation system. No movies. Wee seats. For food, a small snack in a sack. And even when you think you've got a ticket, you might get bumped to Kalamazoo. Eternal *insecurity*. And yet the dudes at your door are—99.9% of the time—part of this "great crowd" who are showing their faithfulness to "Jehovah's organization" by going door-to-door spreading the "good news" of the Watchtower. Doesn't seem like very good news, does it?

The Bopponautic Spaceboat

Members of the Heaven's Gate cult seemed like quiet, clean-cut, vaguely Christian computer nerds until they laced up their new Nikes, shed their bodily "containers" in group suicide, and tried to soar to a higher existence on a spaceship trailing Comet Hale-Bopp. Then the world caught up with what the Bopponauts really believed—another glimpse into what a cult teaches about how to get to God.

Heaven's Gaters used a load of Christian terms, but their version of Jesus and what he accomplished for the human race sounded nothing like the Bible. Their leader, Marshall Applewhite, claimed to be a replacement for Jesus and attempted to strip away Jesus' identity as the Son of God who died in our place. As the supposed representative of the "Kingdom Level Above Human," Applewhite was the sole "shepherd" who could lead humans to a higher level of life. No one could hitch a ride to heaven but with him.

Applewhite mocked people who could "graciously accept death with the hope that through [Christ's] shed blood, or some other equally worthless religious precept, you will go to Heaven after your death." The Heaven's Gaters promised a spacecraft would swoop down for anyone who joined them—joined them through suicide, that is, preferably from the southwestern United States. (You gotta wonder why just the southwest. To save space gas? Or is there something special about dirt, rocks, lizards, and cacti?)

The press release they left behind told how to win their version of salvation: "The requirement is to not only believe who the Representatives are, but *to do as they and we did*. . . . This includes the ultimate sacrifice and demonstration of faith—that is, *the shedding of your human body*." Heaven's Gaters ditched Jesus and made suicide and spaceships the way to eternal bliss.

Don't try that at home.

It was a limited-time offer.

But a bunch of people bought it.

And whoops—they forgot the fine print: No refunds. All sales are final. REALLY final.

Be on the Lookout

Cults make the impossible sound believable. They pitch a heaven far different from what the Bible reveals. Most important, they sell you a plan to save yourself. All cults try to sneak *you* into the process of salvation.

They might as well tell you to jump over the Grand Canyon. "Just leap and you'll have it made. There's a nice soft airbag right over there—twenty miles away on the North Rim." Very comforting. And totally useless. You'll go *splatto* roughly ten feet out and two thousand feet down. No far-off landing zone—no matter how cushy—will keep your body from bursting like a bag of SpaghettiOs.

Saving yourself is the *mission impossible* gospel plan. Don't count on it.

Here are a couple clear points on how cults err in their plan of salvation—goofing on the prize you win and the process of being saved by God.

Cults replace grace with human merit. Grace is about the coolest word in the Bible. It's God's favor toward those who not only don't deserve his mercy but who actually deserve his anger. Since grace comes *completely* from God, there's simply no room for a human boost or boast (1 Corinthians 1:30–31). People don't like that—well, at least people who haven't confessed faith in the true and living Lord Jesus. So they find ways to replace grace and faith with a fake religion that makes them feel better about themselves.

Cults say faith alone won't cut it. While the Bible is plain in saying that faith in Jesus Christ is the only way to be saved (Ephesians 2:8–10; John 5:24), the cults all tweak the simple truth of the Gospel. Many actually mock the idea that faith in Christ is "enough." Get this straight: Grace is free, but it isn't cheap. It's what brought Jesus Christ from the halls of

WHAT'S WITH THE DUDES AT THE DOOR?

heaven to a stable in Bethlehem, and then to a rough and painful cross.

One Way to Paradise

Cults always push someone or something other than Jesus as Savior. That shouldn't surprise us. Even in the first days of the Church people did the same thing. Paul, in fact, wrote a whole book—his letter to the Galatians—to combat people who forget that salvation is a pure gift. He wrote to people he feared were trying to impress God rather than trust their acceptance because of Christ's death. What Paul wrote shows the seriousness of skipping Christ for some other plan. Hot stuff:

> I am astonished that you are so quickly deserting the one who called you by the grace of Christ and are turning to a different gospel—which is really no gospel at all. Evidently some people are throwing you into confusion and are trying to pervert the gospel of Christ. But even if we or an angel from heaven should preach a gospel other than the one we preached to you, let him be eternally condemned! (Galatians 1:6–8)

Those are harsh words for anyone who departs from simple faith in Christ as the way to be saved. God wasn't going to ground those folks for a day. They were grounded for the rest of eternity.

And that's not the prize they wanted.

Think About This Stuff:

1. What does God promise those who know him through Jesus Christ? Why are Christian beliefs about Jesus so frequently attacked?

2. What does Mormonism promise its faithful followers? What does it teach about Jesus and salvation?

3. In Mormonism, how does a person get right with God?

4. Contrast what Christianity teaches about salvation with what Mormonism teaches (hint: check out the chart).

5. If you were a Jehovah's Witness, what would you think about eternity and heaven?

6. Why did the Heaven's Gate cult miss the spiritual space-boat?

7. What false things should you look for in what cults teach about the Gospel—God's Good News?

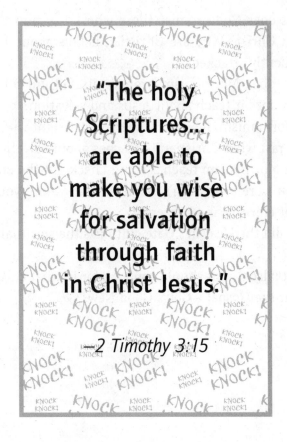

"The holy Scriptures... are able to make you wise for salvation through faith in Christ Jesus."

—2 Timothy 3:15

Who'd Name Their Kid Moroni?

chapter 7

Zeezrom. Amulek. Alma. To Mormon kids these *Book of Mormon* heroes are as familiar as Paul, John, or Mary are to Christian kids. After all, if you'd grown up in a Mormon home playing with Moroni action figures, these names would sound no more funky than Nephi, Omni, Helaman, or Ether. But ponder this: Weirdness cuts both ways. Any non-Christian reading about Hosea or Habbakuk for the first time no doubt finds Bible names strange, too. It all depends on what you're used to.

The point? You can't evaluate someone else's faith by what *seems* strange. The contents of the book of Revelation spook plenty of people—in fact, they startle Christians, too. How anyone *feels* about something isn't vitally important. It's whether that something is *true* or not that matters.

A few chapters back we saw how the Bible is the ultimate uncovering of God's truth. It's God's Word. Our final source of authority. The final word in an argument. The Big Kahuna of truth standards. It's "God-breathed." It's God talking to you, first person. It's God's utterly unique utterances.

The cults, though, aren't happy letting the Bible speak for itself. How could they be? If they taught the obvious meaning of the Bible, nobody would buy what they say, since they teach things that directly contradict the Bible—or at the least go way beyond what the Bible actually says. So they're forced to find ways around the Bible.

How to Cook Up a Cult

Cults seldom hold people hostage. They rarely wield an irresistible mind control that robs members of their ability to choose for or against their system of beliefs. But the confusing teachings of cults do put peoples' brains on spin cycle. A cult, in fact, can develop a loyal following if it's got just two ingredients coming together in a persuasive mix. A cult needs a *leader*, and it needs a fresh *source of authority*, most often some type of revered writings.

Cult Ingredient #1: Start With a Hot Leader

When you study how cults get started, you notice something. Every cult needs a powerful leader-type guy—or gal, in the case of groups like Christian Science and a few others—right at the start. This strong personality claims special insight into God's truth and convinces others he knows what he's talking about. Founders of cults are usually good organizers but even better communicators. People gather round because of the force of their speaking and personality, and they manage to build a following.

Take Joseph Smith, founder of Mormonism. Though Smith wasn't well schooled, he was a good communicator. The guy could spin a tale. His mom said he would fascinate the family for hours at night with tales of the ancient inhabitants of the Americas—how they dressed, how they fought their wars, all sorts of things. And he was doing this years before he came up with the *Book of Mormon*.

Other cults grew up around people who could gather a crowd—even if it's a small crowd. It really wasn't how *many* people, but rather the idea that this leader sounds like he knows what he's talking about. *You* may not want to get married by Sun Myung Moon (the Unification Church—the Moonies) in a mass ceremony with 30,000 other couples, but *somebody* listens to him. Same with Mary Baker Eddy (Christian Science) or David Koresh (Branch Davidians). *You* might not find them persuasive, but others do.

Leaders don't live forever, though. For a cult to survive, it also needs a second leader, someone ready to step in and keep the movement alive after the big guy dies. If the cult has that kind of leader, the group survives. If it lacks that leader, it's done. When Joseph Smith was murdered in 1844, for example, Brigham Young took over the movement. While there was a split right afterward—common in emerging cults—most of Smith's followers stuck with Young. Though he wasn't nearly as colorful a character as Smith, Young was charismatic enough to keep the Mormon movement alive. In the same way, leadership of the Watchtower Bible and Tract Society (Jehovah's Witnesses) passed from Charles Taze Russell to Judge Rutherford. Both men were rousing speakers, and Rutherford took what Russell had started and continued to push the claims of the Witnesses.

Ingredient #2: Bake Up a Fresh Bible

Cults always believe God has bequeathed to their leader a special ability to interpret the Bible—to see something in the Bible that two thousand years' worth of Christians have been too dumb to figure out. When the cult leader speaks, people swarm to listen. His lectures or writings become words people live by—virtual Scripture. And sometimes cult leaders even go a step further and claim to give us actual new Scriptures—sort of a souped-up, modernized Bible that just happens to provide tidy answers to all the tough questions we argue about. What happens, of course, is that this "new revelation" ends up winning the battle of the Bibles within the cult, making the *real* Bible little more than a stumbling bump.

Joseph Smith and the *Book of Mormon*

A prime example of how new Scriptures come along—and how the Bible gets dropped to second, or third, or fourth place—is found in Mormonism. Back in the rip-roaring world of the 1820s in upper New York state, Joseph Smith claimed an angel had led him to a spot where golden plates were buried. When the angel finally let him take possession of these plates, they came complete with big old spectacles—glasses, basically—that allowed him to "translate" the unknown language they were written in.

The result of this "translation" process was the *Book of Mormon*. Alleged to contain the ancient history of the Americas, the *Book of Mormon* claims American Indians are descendants of Israelites who migrated to the Americas prior to the destruction of Jerusalem in 586 B.C. When they arrived, these Israelites split into good guys (the Nephites, pronounced like *knee-fights*) and bad guys (the Lamanites, pronounced *lame-an-ites*). They fought all sorts of battles, and they managed to have lots of the same things happen to them that happened to characters in the Bible. Eventually God cursed the bad guys and gave them dark skin (leading to a long history of racism in the Mormon Church).

To make a rambling story short, Jesus, upon his death in Jerusalem, came to the Americas, established his Church, and chose twelve apostles. (By the way, he also allegedly did a genie-type make-a-wish thing for the disciples. Three of them asked to live until he returned, and so Mormons believe there is a trio of two-*thousand*-year-olds running around America. Maybe they're the dudes at your door.) For a while after Jesus appeared, the Lamanites and Nephites stopped fighting, but in time they got back at it. Eventually the evil, dark-skinned Lamanites wiped out the good, light-skinned Nephites, the final battle conveniently taking place at the Hill Cumorah, a small, non-descript hill close to Joseph Smith's home. The last Nephites were wiped out in A.D. 421, and the last Nephite, who was named Moroni, buried the golden plates that ·recorded the history of preceding generations in the Hill Cumorah. Fourteen hundred years later the man Moroni, now an angel, pointed Joseph Smith to the plates.

Sequels to the *Book of Mormon*

Smith got used to the idea of being a prophet. He began receiving more and more "revelations," which are found in another book of LDS Scripture, the *Doctrine and Covenants*. That's the book where you find the majority of real Mormon doctrine, since the *Book of Mormon* doesn't teach much of what modern Mormons believe about God and salvation.

What do you do when you've got four books of Scripture like the Mormons do? Well, one of them is going to outshine the others, and for Mormons it's normally the *Book of Mormon*. That's the one their leaders constantly encourage them to read and read and read again. When it comes down to a battle of authorities—the Bible versus the *Book of Mormon*—the *Book of Mormon* wins hands down. Mormons simply know it and trust it more than the Bible.

Of course, there are some incredibly basic reasons why Christians (and Mormons!) shouldn't view the *Book of Mormon* as Scripture. Historically, we have an *eensy weensy* problem finding any evidence of the existence of folks called "Nephites" or "Lamanites." Neither can linguists find any trace of the alleged original language of "Reformed Egyptian." The people known to have lived in the Americas at the time the *Book of Mormon* claims to address look nothing like those described in the book. Joseph Smith had them tooling around in horse-drawn chariots and swashbuckling with steel swords—all stuff the folks on this continent knew nothing of until the Spanish showed up a good thousand years later.

Add to that Smith's personal lack of credibility and the contradictions that exist between the Bible and the *Book of Mormon* and you've got good reason to place the *Book of Mormon* on the fiction shelf. These issues aren't just Christians bulldozing the holy hill of Mormonism. They're doubts raised by a wide variety of students of religion.

If You Made Up a Bible

So what makes Mormons swallow these books as sacred words from God? It's a commitment to a *system* and to a *person*. Mormons will offer you "testimonies" to assure you they *know* that Joseph Smith was a prophet—and hence the *Book of Mormon* is for real—and that the current President of the LDS Church is a prophet, too. For many, the argument spins in circles: The *Book of Mormon* is from God because a true prophet gave it, and Joseph Smith is a true prophet because God says so. And so on.

Actually, it takes conniving creative genius to get people to believe you've written a new Bible. You have to cook up new characters. A fresh setting. An original plot. Then you have to juice it up with riveting drama. Problem is, most solidly grounded Christians can smell Scripture fraud as soon as it wafts around their nostrils. They automatically reject "new" revelations and "other" books of Scripture. In fact, to most non-Mormons those golden books allegedly translated from an unknown language with magic spectacles seem more than a little farfetched.

A more devious way to cook up a cult is to simply *reinterpret* the Scripture we already have. It's far easier to sell "This is what the Bible *really* says" than "This is the *new* Bible you really need." What makes it a cinch is that lots of Christians are already in the bad habit of reading the Bible and picking parts they like and parts they don't—or parts they'll obey and parts they won't.

It's a Whole New World

This far more dangerous approach—reinterpreting Scripture—is used by the Watchtower Bible and Tract Society (Jehovah's Witnesses), a popular cult that has grown large in the United States. The Witnesses don't have other books of Scripture. They tell you, in fact, that they believe in the Bible and the Bible alone. They tell you the Bible is perfect, inspired, sufficient—and that they are entirely legit when it comes to Scripture. It all sounds great until they get their Bibles out and you start looking at verses. Then it goes weird.

Jehovah's Witnesses have their own version of the Bible, *The New World Translation* (NWT). This "translation" was published in the early 1950s. The Watchtower Society makes it available cheaply to its members, even providing study editions and a Greek interlinear (an edition with the Greek New Testament and the NWT together). Witnesses genuinely believe the NWT is the best Bible version around, a translation of the New Testament's original Greek far superior to anything used in Christian churches. But the NWT isn't a translation as much as it is a perversion. Whenever a passage pops up where the Bible disagrees with Watchtower teachings—*poofo!*—the NWT "translates" the passage differently.

At this point your brain should scream DANGER! DANGER! If you can't trust what's on a page of the Bible, you can't trust what it means for your life. If you aren't sure what the Bible says, you can't be sure about the God you follow. A couple examples:

The Bible teaches that Jesus Christ is God the Son come as a human being. Jehovah's Witnesses deny that Christ is God. Take a gander at this passage on the deity of Christ:

> For in Him all the fullness of Deity dwells in bodily form. (Colossians 2:9, NASB—a trustworthy translation accepted by all kinds of Christians and scholars).

Because it is in him that all the fulness of the divine
quality dwells bodily. (Colossians 2:9, NWT)

What's a "divine quality"? Being nice? Being big? The
Greek word means "deity" or "what makes God, God." It's a
strong, faith-building term, but you'd never know it reading
the NWT.

Here's another one, probably the verse Jehovah's Witnesses are most famous for twisting:

In the beginning was the Word, and the Word was
with God, and the Word was God. (John 1:1, NASB)

In [the] beginning the Word was, and the Word was
with God, and the Word was a god. (John 1:1, NWT)

Don't try to talk to a Jehovah's Witness about this passage without a library of reference works beside you and a
Greek scholar holding your hand. The Witnesses have been
fed all sorts of false information about this passage, and
they'll repeat it to you with such confidence that it starts to
sound right even though it isn't. If a first-year Greek student
wrote "a god" on a *quizzo* he'd get a big *wrongo*. John never
meant Jesus was "a god." John didn't believe in little "g"
gods. And that's why all modern translations done by teams
of real scholars don't translate it "a god." But JWs have been
told that this is the right way to translate the passage.

Sometimes they get downright devious on you, even *de-
leting* little words that matter hugely for the meaning.
Here's a tricky one. Watch closely:

"If you ask Me anything in My name, I will do it."
(John 14:14, NASB)

"If YOU ask anything in my name, I will do it."
(John 14:14, NWT)

Did you see the word vanish? Jesus said, "If you ask *ME* anything in My name." But the NWT deletes the word "me," even though it's found in the Greek text they publish and distribute to their followers! Why? The passage refers to praying to Jesus. Since the Watchtower doesn't believe Jesus is God, they wretch at the idea of people *praying* to him. So even though their Greek New Testament contains the word, they rewrite the passage.

Trickier Still

A cult doesn't have to call it a "Bible" or a "Book of Anything" or "Scripture" to have another standard that ends up replacing the Bible. The "Mind Science" groups (like Christian Science and Religious Science) all have their own texts you *must have* to really make sense of the Bible. In every instance the cults have a guru, a supreme dude or dudette who got a special insight and put it all down in a book you need to carry right along with the Bible. It becomes the road map that leads you through the Bible.

The First Church of Christ, Scientist (Christian Science), for example, has this question on their web page: "Does *Science and Health with Key to the Scriptures* [a book written by their founder, Mary Baker Eddy] replace the Bible for you?" The answer is revealing: "No. *Science and Health* is a companion to the Bible, and as its title implies, a key to understanding the Scriptures. These two books are the textbooks of Christian Science. . . ."

Big red warning lights should flash when you read something like that. Watch out for anyone who claims special authority or unique abilities to interpret the Bible *even if they still claim to use the Bible and don't teach overly wacky stuff.* Any legitimate Christian scholar recognizes that he or she is one of *many* who speak truth—who teach the core of big stuff the Church has always taught. Anyone who chucks the Bible as final authority is headed into deep doo-doo. Anyone who claims to be able to match wits with the Master of the Universe is headed for a fall. *Science and Health*, for example, doesn't strive to clarify the Bible, as real Bible tools strive to do. It *adds* new truths that contradict the Bible. And Christian Scientists clearly make *Science and Health* their authority for faith.

Be on the Lookout

Some cool tools send you hiking back to the store for more pieces. Some trick toys send you scurrying back for pricey accessories.

The Bible isn't like that. You can call it *complete.* You can call it *reliable.* You can even call it *completely reliable.* Jude put it this way: He urged his readers to "contend for the faith that was once for all entrusted to the saints" (Jude 1:3). What's that mean? Stick up for what you know. And what you need to know about faith God has put in the Bible. If he didn't write it out for you—or if he didn't give you the brainpower or basic Bible tools to figure it out—then it doesn't hit too high on his list of really important stuff.

No one can stop cultic groups from offering funky versions of God. But when they ditch the Bible, they've ditched the clarity of true Christianity. Watch out for these traits:

Cults avoid the plain meaning of Scripture. God didn't stammer when he gave us his Word. But it's amazing what people do to avoid the mondo obvious teachings in the Bible. When you see someone twisting Scripture, avoiding the it-doesn't-take-a-rocket-scientist-to-get-this meaning of the words, you know they've got a problem, and they're probably going to ask you to buy into their ideas.

That doesn't mean you don't use your noggin when you read the Bible. Or that you don't have to compare verse with verse to make sense of the whole Bible. You can tell, though, when someone is doing the "Macarena" around a text. Don't join the dance.

Cults slam the church at large. Cults maintain that nobody before them—or almost nobody, anyway—has gotten faith right. Even though Jesus promised to be with his people forever. Even though Jesus said his Church, founded upon the rock of faith in him, would never fail (Matthew 16:18). Cults like to say that *all* churches have been "corrupted" or "gone astray" or become "apostate." Because some churches *have* gone astray, they figure *all of them* have. Try that logic in another arena: It makes as much sense to say that since there are *some* rotten players on your school's basketball team that *all* the players stink.

Cults rely on one person or a select group of people to interpret what the Bible says. The cults don't allow you to go to God's Word directly and take responsibility for your faith and your beliefs. It's sort of "Here's the menu. Eat it or starve."

Problem is, God makes each one of us responsible to seek truth. And he doesn't let you blame someone else if you mess up on the important questions on his Great Final

Exam—the GFE, a test far more important than the SAT or even the GRE. You can't whine and say, "Hey, but Mr. Prophet Guy said to believe this" or "Mrs. Prophetess Lady taught me this." *Bzzzzt*. Wrong answer. You're responsible for *you*. That means *you* have to learn the Word. *You* are told to "Test everything. Hold on to the good" (1 Thessalonians 5:21). God puts pastors and teachers and other leaders in your life to help, guide, and teach you. But when crunch time comes, he holds *you* responsible for what you believe.

A Whole Buncha Nothin'

The final tip-off that you're dealing with bad dudes: Cults major on minors.

By now you know the big stuff of Christian faith: Who God is, what he's done in Jesus, and how we know. When a teacher makes anything more important than those majors, watch out.

True, sometimes sincere Christians experience bouts of temporary stupidity and forget what's important. But when groups consistently make minor issues major, keep your head together and think straight. Ask yourself this: Has God said this teaching or doctrine will keep me out of heaven if I don't believe it?

Probably not.

And you don't wanna die for a buncha nothin'.

Think About This Stuff:

1. What's the difference between a teaching being *strange* and being *false*?

2. What ingredients does it take to cook up a cult?
3. What is the *Book of Mormon*? What is its basic plotline? Why won't Christians accept the *Book of Mormon* as Scripture?
4. How do Jehovah's Witnesses distort the Bible? Give two examples of twisted Scriptures.
5. What traits should you watch out for in how cults handle the Bible?

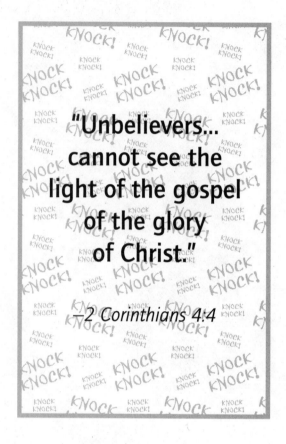

"Unbelievers...
cannot see the
light of the gospel
of the glory
of Christ."

—2 Corinthians 4:4

A Quickie Cult Catalog

chapter 8

You don't grow your own corn.

You don't catch your own cows.

You don't have to figure out cults all by yourself.

Before we wrap up *What's With the Dudes at the Door?* with some news you can truly use—how to cult-proof yourself (chapter 9) and your world (chapter 10)—take time to get familiar with the basic beliefs of the cults listed below. Each is one you're likely to bump into in person or at least in the news. The entries are straightforward: Up top are details like the group's headquarters, its beginnings, and the number of members it claims. The "Main Problem" section describes how the group contradicts basic Christian beliefs about God, Jesus, and the Bible. "Other Stuff to Know" explains, well, other stuff you should know. Groups are listed alphabetically by their formal names, with their familiar names in parentheses. Mormons, for example, appear like this: The Church of Jesus Christ of Latter-day Saints (Mormons).

The Baha'i Faith

Headquarters: Haifa, Israel

Founded: About 1863 by Mirza Husayn' Ali, known to adherents of Baha'i as Bahá'u'lláh.

Current Membership: The Baha'i Faith claims five million members worldwide.

Main Problem: The Baha'i Faith teaches the unity of all of humankind and all religions. A cult of Islamic origin, Baha'i claims to glean the high points of Christianity and all other religions to form one faith.

To quote their own literature, "Bahá'u'lláh taught that there is one God Who progressively reveals His will to humanity. Each of the great religions brought by the Messengers of God—Moses, Buddha, Krishna, Jesus, Muhammad, Zoroaster—represents a successive stage in the spiritual development of civilization. Bahá'u'lláh, the most recent Messenger in this line, has brought teachings that address the moral and spiritual challenges of the modern world." Hence, Jesus is but one of many "Messengers of God." The fact that each of these "messengers" taught something quite different than the others—Moses and Jesus being the exception to the rule—doesn't bother Baha'is. Consistency of beliefs isn't their strong point.

Doctrines like the Trinity, deity of Christ, salvation by grace through faith, and the like aren't so much *denied* as made less important than a forget-all-differences unity. The Baha'i Faith is highly eclectic, drawing from all other religions, resulting in a jumbled theology.

The revelations of Bahá'u'lláh supercede the Bible or any other religious writing.

Other Stuff to Know: Baha'is are widely active on college campuses. Their let's-all-get-along attitude toward truth makes them effective recruiters.

The Church of Christ, Scientist (Christian Science)

Headquarters: Boston, Massachusetts

Founded: 1879 by Mary Baker Eddy, "the Discoverer, Founder, and Leader of Christian Science."

Current Membership: Approximately 150,000 members worldwide.

Main Problem: In Christian Science, there is no real, personal God.

God is called "Divine Principle, Life, Truth, Love, Soul, Spirit, Mind" (*Science and Health*, p. 115). Only spirit is real. The material world is unreal—meaning disease, sickness, pain, suffering, and evil are all *illusions*.

Christian Science denies the central doctrines of the Christian faith: the Trinity, the deity of Christ, the separate and eternal personhood of the Spirit, bodily resurrection, the Atonement (Christ's sacrificial death for us), and salvation by grace through faith. Human beings are "God's spiritual idea, individual, perfect, eternal."

While using some of the same terminology as true Christians, Christian Science so radically redefines faith's starting points that the final product isn't even remotely similar to real Christian belief.

Other Stuff to Know: A number of "Mind Science" groups hold similar doctrines: Religious Science, Divine Science, Unity School of Christianity, Science of Mind, and the Church of Religious Science.

Since Christian Science denies the reality of pain, suffering, and disease, members traditionally haven't believed in using medical procedures, such as medicine or surgery, that the rest of society takes for granted. Since everything is caused by spiritual rather than physical realities, they believe all healing must come from the spiritual realm. Some practitioners of Christian Science have been prosecuted for refusing to obtain medical treatment for a child who later died of a treatable disease.

The Church of Jesus Christ of Latter-day Saints (Mormons)

Headquarters: Salt Lake City, Utah

Founded: April 6, 1830 (the date most Mormons believe is Jesus' birthday) by Joseph Smith and a small group of others.

Current Membership: Official LDS membership passed the ten million mark in November 1997. Because of aggressive overseas missionary activity, there are now more Mormons outside the United States than inside it. It is one of the world's fastest-growing religious groups.

Main Problem: Wrong God. Wrong Jesus. Wrong Gospel.

The Mormon God (Elohim) is an exalted man from another planet; his firstborn spirit son is Jesus Christ. All other humans are spirit children of this exalted man and his many wives in heaven. Mormonism says God and man are of the same "species," directly contradicting the Bible (Isaiah 29:16). Jesus, according to Mormonism, hasn't eternally been God, and some Mormons even believe Jesus won't receive the "fullness of exaltation" until he takes wives and has children during the millennium, a thousand-year period at the end of time. The gospel in Mormonism focuses on the goal of becoming a god and progressing up the ladder of exaltation, putting the focus on human beings rather than God.

Other Stuff to Know: Besides the Bible, Mormons have three books they regard as Scripture: the *Book of Mormon,* the *Doctrine and Covenants*, and *The Pearl of Great Price*. They claim to have a living Prophet (who heads the LDS Church), twelve Apostles (key leaders of the movement akin to Jesus' disciples), and a restored priesthood (a leadership structure to which most male Mormons belong).

Mormons claim that all Christian churches abandoned true Christianity in the second century, and the true church had to be "restored" under Joseph Smith.

Mormons build temples where they perform ceremonies necessary for individuals to become gods. Ceremonies include "eternal marriage," which "seals" a woman to her husband "for time and eternity," and "endowment." In endowment, temple participants put on temple garments, make covenants, and watch films portraying topics including the creation and the fall. Before the temple ceremonies underwent major changes in April 1990, Christian ministers and Christian theology were mocked in the LDS endowment ceremony.

International Churches of Christ (Boston Church)

Headquarters: Formerly known as Crossroads Church of Christ. First located in Boston, Massachusetts, the ICoC

WHAT'S WITH THE DUDES AT THE DOOR?

later moved to Los Angeles, California.

Founded: 1979 by Kip McKean, Bob Gempel, and others, with about thirty people.

Current Membership: The Los Angeles group alone averages more than 10,000 attendees for Sunday services. The ICoC is growing at a phenomenal rate. They currently boast more than 155,000 people in attendance in 312 churches in 124 different countries.

Main Problem: The International Churches of Christ don't deny the Trinity or the deity of Christ or the person of the Holy Spirit, making it harder to spot the group's cultic traits. They confess "orthodox" things like the Trinity and even speak of salvation by grace through faith. Yet they plainly teach that a person must not only be baptized to be saved—a view known as "baptismal regeneration"—but be "discipled."

The ICoC's concept of discipleship is far different from that of other Christians, emphasizing the idea so strongly that they cross the line into unbiblical teaching. Discipleship is something you *must* do to be saved and to stay saved, becoming a works system added to the finished work of Christ. In other words, it's the grace thing—in the ICoC, grace ends up taking a backseat.

Other Stuff to Know: While ICoC doctrines *may* be technically correct, they seem to be guilty of "exclusivism," thinking that they alone are true Christians. That's about six notches past arguing your church has the best understanding of Christian truth. What's more, many people—including leaders of the traditional mainline Churches of Christ—have identified the ICoC as a cultic group using discipling techniques that smack of mind control. Time will tell whether members of the ICoC are hyperactive Christians or deceived cultists. In the meantime, stay clear.

Tremendously active in recruiting on college campuses, the ICoC has been banned from at least one campus for its less-than-up-front outreach techniques.

Oneness Pentecostalism ("Jesus Only")

Headquarters: The largest Oneness Pentecostal group, the United Pentecostal Church, is headquartered in Hazelwood, Missouri. Similar groups include various "Apostolic" and "Jesus Only" churches.

Founded: Oneness Pentecostalism in its modern forms broke off from mainline Pentecostal groups around 1916. Their denial of the Trinity, though, is one of the earliest heresies in the Church and dates way back to the second century.

Current Membership: Difficult to determine because of the number of groups that would fall into this category. They currently claim a worldwide following of 2.3 million people.

Main Problem: Jesus Only folks deny the doctrine of the Trinity. For them, God is one Person. Some say that the Father is the Son, the Son is the Spirit, and the Spirit is the Father. God, in other words, is like an actor on a stage— sometimes wearing the "Father" mask, sometimes wearing the "Son" mask, and sometimes wearing the "Spirit" mask. Others say the Father is the true deity, the Son is just a human being indwelt by the Father, and the Spirit is just another term for the Father. However they express their beliefs, Oneness Pentecostals don't believe there are three eternal Persons—the Father, the Son, and the Spirit.

Other Stuff to Know: Most Oneness groups heavily emphasize baptism and speaking in tongues as things absolutely necessary to salvation. And they also believe it is completely wrong to baptize in the name of the Father, Son, and Holy Spirit (Matthew 28:19). Genuine baptism, they say, is "only" in the name of Jesus.

The Unification Church (Moonies)

Headquarters: New York, New York

Founded: 1954 by Sun Myung Moon.

Current Membership: The Unification Church *claims* as many as three million followers worldwide, with some 45,000 in the United States. Real membership, however, is probably far below this number. Membership has declined over the past decade from highs reached in the '70s and '80s.

Main Problem: Sun Myung Moon, who calls himself the "Lord of the Second Advent," believes he is the new Messiah—essentially, a modern replacement for Jesus.

Moon's teachings are wildly unChristian. Aside from denying the Trinity, the true deity of Christ, and many other Christian teachings, Moon adds a number of beliefs that are several notches past startling, some of which aren't fit to mention here.

In short, Moon claims that Jesus failed in his true mission and that Jesus' death on the cross was settling for mere "spiritual" redemption. The mantle has passed to Moon, the Lord of the Second Advent, to complete the process of saving humanity.

This he does in a most unusual way. What Jesus failed

to do, Moon claims, was to marry and have children. Moon—together with the perfect bride, Mrs. Moon—has provided for humanity's *physical* salvation. (Never mind Moon's convictions for bigamy and promiscuity in Korea— apparently while searching for Mrs. Right.) Moon and his wife have produced thirteen "sinless" children and regard themselves as the "True Parents" of humanity. Moon now performs huge marriage ceremonies of his followers—with 300,000 couples linked by satellite in 1995. Moon promises that couples married by him will have sinless children of their own, bequeathing salvation in a most unusual manner.

The remainder of Moon's theology is a mishmash of Eastern religions, Christian terminology, and occultism. He speaks of having contacted spirits in seances.

The main source of written authority for the Unification Church is Moon's book *The Divine Principle*, which functions as the Bible for the Moonies.

Other Stuff to Know: Moonies, best known for their hey-buddy-would-you-like-to-buy-a-flower fund-raising in airport terminals, own the influential *Washington Times* newspaper, just one piece of a financial empire ranging from soft-drink companies to weapons manufacturers. The powerful, politically conservative Moonies have come a long way from their reputation as one of the worst brainwashing cults of the 1970s.

Unitarian-Universalism

Headquarters: Boston, Massachusetts

Founded: The current Unitarian-Universalist Association (UUA) grew out of the consolidation and merger in

1963 of two denominations; those previous groups were founded in 1793 and 1825.

Current Membership: About 205,000 members currently attend UUA churches. However, due to the liberal, loose-knit character of the group, nearly twice that number would identify themselves with the Unitarian-Universalist view in the United States alone.

Main Problem: While presenting little in the way of a positive theology, the UUA undercuts the Bible, the Trinity, the deity of Christ, salvation by grace through faith, and basically all Christian beliefs.

The UUA is aggressively anti-Christian, cloaking this stance under the guise of "acceptance" and "unity." "Unitarian" signals the group's rejection of the Trinity; "Universalist" implies that all people will be saved from God's final judgment.

Other Stuff to Know: The UUA illustrates how a group that long ago considered itself biblical and Christian could devolve into radical liberal theology and then into anti-Christian cultism.

Watch for UUA opinions in secular news media—on everything from gay rights to environmental issues to evangelism. Despite its ditching of biblical faith, the UUA gets positive press coverage as a respectable Christian denomination. A larger than normal percentage of UUA adherents are found in college and university teaching positions.

The Watchtower Bible and Tract Society (Jehovah's Witnesses)

Headquarters: Brooklyn, New York
Founded: About 1884 by Charles Taze Russell.

Current Membership: The Watchtower doesn't keep membership rolls. Instead, they track how many people attend and participate in their yearly "Memorial" (what Christians call the Lord's Supper) and how many people witness door-to-door. Based on these numbers, about ten to fifteen million people follow the teachings of the Watchtower Society worldwide.

Main Problems: Denial of the deity of Christ and the Holy Spirit. Denial of Christ's bodily resurrection from the grave. Faulty doctrine of salvation.

The Watchtower Society teaches that there is one true God, Jehovah. In his first creative act, he made Michael the Archangel. Through Michael he created everything else. In JW theology, Michael becomes Jesus Christ—well, sort of. The Holy Spirit (always written "holy spirit" in Watchtower literature) is not a person but an "impersonal active force." The Society therefore denies the Trinity, the full equality of the three persons of the godhood—Father, Son, and Spirit. They admit that the term "god" is used of Jesus but believe he is a lesser being than Jehovah. They are, therefore, not monotheists (believers in one true God).

The Watchtower denies that Jesus rose bodily from the grave, teaching that Jehovah "re-created" Michael the Archangel and somehow disposed of Jesus' body. Some Witnesses believe Jesus' body still exists somewhere as a memorial to God's love, while others think Jehovah dissolved it into gases.

Witnesses also have a gospel that divides the "saved" into two groups: the "anointed class" of 144,000 literal individuals, and the "great crowd" of all other Witnesses. Only the anointed go to heaven; the rest live forever in a paradise earth. Only about seven or eight thousand of the anointed class are still alive, so the vast majority of Jehovah's Witnesses have an "earthly hope" rather than a "heavenly hope." Those in the great crowd have a second-class salvation: no personal relationship with Jesus, no prayer to Jesus, no participation in the New Covenant, no full and complete justification in him. They enjoy Jesus only as they fellowship with the anointed class.

Other Stuff to Know: The Watchtower publishes its own mistranslation of the Bible, the *New World Translation*. Besides being a truly lousy read, this version alters Bible passage after Bible passage that disagree with Witness beliefs. Its mistranslation of important verses on the deity of Christ, the person of the Holy Spirit, the soul of human beings, etc., makes witnessing to Witnesses very difficult.

The Way International

Headquarters: The main faction of The Way is headquartered in New Knoxville, Ohio. After the 1985 death of The Way's founder, a number of splinter groups formed in other places.

Founded: Victor Paul Wierwille founded the group, tracing the beginning to a radio program that first aired in 1942.

Current Membership: The main group, which follows Wierwille's successor, L. Craig Martindale, has 10,000–20,000 remaining members. These members, however, are actively involved in college campuses recruiting and inviting people to "twig fellowships." Other groups that follow Wierwille's teachings remain active, as well, making the total number of people caught in this doctrinal system at least 50,000 in the U.S. and Canada.

Main Problems: Loosely put, The Way is a charismatic version of Jehovah's Witnesses. Wierwille's teachings are a bit tough to grasp. They deny the Trinity by denying the deity of Christ and the Holy Spirit, at times even using the same "holy spirit" designation as the Witnesses. Unlike the Witnesses, they deny Jesus existed prior to his birth in Bethlehem. Wierwille wrote,

> In other words, I am saying that Jesus Christ is not God, but the Son of God. They are not "co-eternal, without beginning or end, and co-equal." Jesus Christ was not literally with God in the beginning; neither does he have all the assets of God. (*Jesus Christ is Not God*, p. 5, 1981 edition)

This directly contradicts passages that plainly teach Jesus *did* exist prior to his coming to earth in the Incarnation, such as John 1:1 and Colossians 1:15ff. Wierwille taught that these passages referred only to the idea that Jesus existed in the mind of God as an idea, nothing more.

Other Stuff to Know: The Way is very aggressive in making converts. They teach that speaking in tongues is necessary to be saved. Most believe that all churches other than their own are totally corrupt.

Think About This Stuff:

1. Big challenge: For each cult listed, name and explain three points where that cult conflicts with Christianity.
2. Which cults are you most likely to meet in your neighborhood? Where? Which are you likely to find on a college campus?

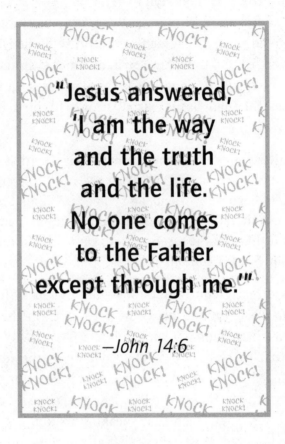

"Jesus answered, 'I am the way and the truth and the life. No one comes to the Father except through me.'"

—John 14:6

chapter 9

How to Avoid Being Swallowed Whole by a Cult

Skating on thin ice.

Skinny-dipping with crocodiles.

Bungee-jumping with rubberbands borrowed from a friend's braces.

Rushing a football with no offensive line.

Strolling down a dark alley in a nasty 'hood while wondering aloud how to spend the three thousand bucks bulging in your pocket.

Wandering with an imaginary purple dinosaur through a pack of velociraptors.

What do all these things have in common?

They're things you avoid if you have a brain.

You stay off thin ice. You swim clear of the crocodile rocks. You bungee-jump only if your mother signs the release form. You flip the football to someone else when no one blocks for you. You keep your mouth shut about your money. And you stay out of the backyard when velociraptors prowl.

Staying clear of cults is just as big a no-brainer.

Some cults are shave-your-head-and-chant outfits. A few make their members white-shirt-and-dark-tie respectable. Or even pinch-your-cheek cute. However weird or wonderful they may look on the outside, cults are *all* spiritually deadly. They swallow you whole. They digest you down to the bone and then dispose of your soul.

That's not a place you want to go.

Here's the problem: No one can perfectly protect you from being swallowed headfirst by a cult. And here's why: Knowing what you believe and staying cult-free is *your* responsibility.

The Cult-Proof Christian

Getting cult-proofed is a bit like going to the doctor to get up-to-date on your shots. You have to get there yourself—you can't send a substitute. You're taking a risk if you don't. A *big* risk. You might not need a shot's disease-fighting immunity right away—but sooner or later it keeps you from getting deathly sick.

But get this good news: The cult-proofing process isn't so painful. By now you've already got most of what you need. And the experience won't give you nightmares where you get chased by nurses with nine-inch needles. Getting an anti-cult inoculation actually feels good:

- *You get more of God*. The best part of cult-proofing yourself is that you get to know your Lord a whole lot better. Think about it: Studying what the Bible teaches about God—an area where cults whip most Christians— not only helps you recognize cultic error but also gives you a grip on what God is doing in your world and your life.

- *You won't get sold a fake God.* Someone who knows the truth is less likely to get snookered by a lie. Remember? Your first job isn't to memorize a bunch of wrong stuff someone else believes. More important than knowing Joseph Smith's secret eyeglass prescription or the boo-boos the Watchtower Society makes translating New Testament Greek is knowing what *you* believe.

- *You can help your friends when they're confused.* You may figure you'll never fall prey to the cults. Well, you won't—if you're prepared. And if you don't get proud. But knowing what the Bible says about being saved by Jesus helps you share the *real* Gospel with a person trapped in a cult. And it helps you talk to Christian friends who start to waffle on what they believe.

- *You get a solid faith.* Suppose you go to lunch with a friend in your school cafeteria. You go through the line and pick up something the lunch ladies can't wreck—a PB&J sandwich. Your friend grabs something you figure is more risky—say, a crispy meat burrito. Three bites later he's lying dead on the lunchroom floor. You'd feel bad for your friend. But glad you bagged the burrito. You'd resolve once again to steer clear of deep-fried lunch entrees made from unidentified animals.

  Here's a fact: God tastes even better when you know some people are getting slipped bad burritos stuffed with cultic false teachings. The truth about who God is shines bright against the dark backdrop of the cults. Suddenly it matters that you believe in *one God*. That Jesus is *divine*. Maybe for the first time in your life you

133

think about *what eternity will be like*—and you're sure you won't be spending your forever as exalted ruler of your personal planetoid. You discover why you aren't interested in someone else's "Scriptures" and *how important the Bible is* to your everyday life.

- *You stay out of spiritual danger.* Cults have ditched biblical faith. If that was an insignificant Burger King vs. McDonald's kind of choice, no one would care. But cults have chosen another god. And in doing that, they've chosen separation from God—hell—for eternity. Cultists might be the nicest, goodest, friendliest people you know. But they don't know God as God himself has declared he should be known. (Lest you think Christians are exceedingly intolerant, they say *we* are the ones who are lost.)

Want to avoid getting sucked into a cult? Staying safe is your job. Your responsibility. But there are some things you can do to help yourself and others.

The Cult-Proof Christian Knows a Big God

The cults can't trick you with a fake God if you know the real thing. So the better you know God the better off you'll be.

Knowing God, after all, is what your life as a Christian is all about. It starts now. It goes forever. It's your purpose for all of time and the time beyond: "Now this is eternal life," Jesus prayed, "that they may know you, the only true God, and Jesus Christ, whom you have sent" (John 17:3). The Bible says everything you go through in life is supposed to make you more like Christ and reveal God to you so you'll know him better, love him more, and trust him in everything (Romans 8:28). So focusing on God should be no surprise.

You need to know your God. What he's done for you. What he's like. And don't neglect the stuff you may not hear about as often: who he is at the core of his being. If you grasp the material on the Trinity in chapter five well enough to tell it to somebody else, that's the real trick. If you can explain how the Bible teaches that Jesus is God without making Jesus the Father—remember?—you'll not only help that person but get a firm grip on passages in the Bible that would otherwise baffle your brain. Get growing in this biggie of the faith and you'll get cult-proofed, as well.

The Cult-Proof Christian Clings to Jesus

Jesus said this: "I am the vine; you are the branches. If a man remains in me and I in him, he will bear much fruit; apart from me you can do nothing" (John 15:5). No fruit grows by rolling around on the ground by itself. No branch survives on its own. Fruit to branch, branch to stalk, stalk to root—everything is hooked together or it dies. Jesus calls you a branch. He's the plant. You can't exist without him.

Jesus is your protection against fuzzy faith. It's nice to say "I believe in God." But what matters is that you embrace Christ—God in the flesh. Ponder these: The one who knows the Son knows the Father (1 John 2:23). Jesus is "the image of the invisible God" (Colossians 1:15). In Christ "all the fullness of the Deity lives in bodily form" (Colossians 2:9).

Jesus is the world's unique Savior. Jesus claimed this: "I am the way and the truth and the life. No one comes to the

Father but through me" (John 14:6). Strong words. Jesus backed them up by rising from the dead. But people are scared of what Jesus said. If he's right, they have to deal with *him* and with *him alone*. There's no weaseling out of dealing with Christ. He's *it*.

That's why the cults don't like John 14:6. Many cults out-and-out deny that Jesus is the only way. Others swap him for their own stunted version of Jesus, a sort of mini-god or mega-nice-guy. It lets them cook up their own gospel and their own way to heaven. Problem is, the wrong Jesus can't save.

Jesus demands a unique response. God doesn't demand you love him before he'll love you. But loving him—obeying, following, worshiping him—is an appropriate way to say thanks to him. It works like this: "For Christ's love compels us. . . . And he died for all, that those who live should no longer live for themselves but for him who died for them and was raised again" (2 Corinthians 5:14–15). You can't love the One who died to set you free too much.

Get a good dose of who Jesus is.

And of how you can love him in return.

Keep your eyes peeled for the ways cults try to get rid of the real Jesus.

And stick this in the front of your brain: You won't follow the cults if you're busy following Jesus.

The Cult-Proof Christian Gloms to God's Grace

John Newton was twenty-two when he became the master of a slave ship. What a wretched guy—evil beyond words! Shuttling men, women, and children in chains, he treated and traded people like pigs. Surely Newton deserved to be voted *Least Likely to Become a Decent Guy*. But Newton became a Christian. He worked to abolish slavery. And later he wrote these words:

> *Amazing grace, how sweet the sound,*
> *That saved a wretch like me.*
> *I once was lost, but now am found,*
> *Was blind, but now I see.*

Newton discovered that Christ's death was big and bold enough to pay for sins even as looming as his. God's grace scrubbed even a slave trader clean. He must have banged his forehead and said, "Wow! I've been forgiven!"

Grace should amaze you. Every good thing you have, are, or do is given to you by grace. God forgives you. He loves you. Every day of life. No matter what mess you're in. Grace is also what grows you. It teaches you "to deny ungodliness and worldly desires and to live sensibly, righteously and godly in the present age" (Titus 2:12, NASB).

What chaps the cults about grace is this: It sings, "God is great," but says diddly about *us*. It inflates God. It deflates us. Grace lets the air out of all our pride. It says, "You are dependent on God." It gives all the credit to the One to whom it belongs: God. The cult-proof Christian freely admits his or her total need for God.

So whenever you hear *anyone* adding works or anything else to grace, run away! Or prepare to share God's truth and show from Scripture that Paul had it right: "And if by grace, then it is no longer by works; if it were, grace would no longer be grace" (Romans 11:6). And this: "It is BECAUSE OF HIM that you are in Christ Jesus, who has become for us wisdom from God—that is, our righteousness, holiness and redemption. Therefore, as it is written: 'LET HIM WHO BOASTS BOAST IN THE LORD' " (1 Corinthians 1:30–31, whopper emphasis added). Forget those facts and faith is false.

The Cult-Proof Christian Isn't DuhDuhDumb About the Bible

Cults gore you with your ignorance of the Bible. Mormons come along and quote a bunch of obscure verses and *jab jab jab*—they've got you. Even more slyly, Jehovah's Witnesses use your ignorance to pin you on points you never thunk of.

It's a *thump or get thumped* world. Either you know the Word so you can state what you believe, or you get thumped by the cultist with a better grip on the Bible.

Do you love the Bible? Not that absolutely cool edition of the bestselling *TeenAngel Bible* your parents gave you last Christmas—but *the Word*, the stuff *inside* the 100% genuine mooing cowskin binding? Take a second right now and thumb to Psalm 119 in your Bible. You can't miss it. It's huge—biggest chapter in the book, smack in the middle. Read through just a few sections, remembering this is sort of a prayer set to music. Every verse says something about love for God's Word.

Can you pray the way the Psalmist prayed? If you can, then you know what it means to treasure God's Word. If you can't, don't panic. Love grows. Ask God to show you how incredible his Word really is. Start spending time in it daily, not with a wail and a whine but with the same enthusiasm you have for meeting a best friend. And most important, as you "get into the Word," get the Word into you! Memorize. Make the Bible part of you. Hide the Word in your heart (Psalm 119:11). Nothing gives you more confidence in your Christian walk. No other way of studying the Bible cult-proofs you better.

The Cult-Proof Christian Hangs With a Herd

Boys and girls, this next point is definitely TV–14V. But it isn't anything you haven't seen on the Discovery Channel—and it's akin to what humans inflict on Bessie to get those bovine-skin Bibles: *Wolves manage to knock off animals a lot larger than themselves by separating individuals out from the herd.*

Survival of the fittest.

Circle of life.

Food chain facts.

Here's how that ugly reality relates to cults: A Christian who has been separated from the herd of God's people is easy prey for cults. Maybe he wandered off because he got hurt—who hasn't been smashed by God's people? Or she left because church was boring—who hasn't wheezed through a snoozer sermon? Cults shower that person with concern and compassion, and before long they've got another faithful follower. Happens all the time.

No church is perfect. Nope—you don't want First Church of the Forever Frozen. God is cool—not frozen. Nor do you need Swinging Chandelier Christian Center. Jesus will energize you—but he shouldn't need a spatula to scrape you off the ceiling.

But lots of churches will grow you God's way. Paul explains how church is supposed to work. To each one of us, he says, "grace has been given as Christ apportioned it" (Ephesians 4:7). Christ has given each of us a hunk of grace. But he means a specific grace. What's *this* grace for? "It was he who gave some to be apostles, some to be prophets, some to be evangelists, and some to be pastors and teachers" (Ephesians 4:11). God made each of us different—each with a "spiritual gift" that will benefit the church. A church that is functioning tells non-Christians about Jesus. It cares for hurts. It teaches truth. Listen to what happens when we herd together: Paul says we're prepared to serve, we're hooked together like parts in a body, we get unified around Jesus, and we become mature (Ephesians 4:12–13).

Then Paul goes graphic. If we don't hang together, we're like infants "tossed back and forth by the waves, and blown here and there by every wind of teaching and by the cunning and craftiness of men in their deceitful scheming" (Ephesians 4:14).

Get those pictures? Animal hunted down. Baby bobbing on ocean.

Not pretty.

Better hang with the herd.

It's Swell to Stay Well

Staying cult-free is like keeping clear of infectious diseases. You scrub to your elbows. You stop breathing when someone sneezes. You move out when your mom gets the flu. You stay away from doorknobs in snot season. And you don't borrow used tissues—even from a friend.

But it's the combined effect of each ingredient in God's innoculation against the cults that does the trick:

Focusing on God—

Following Christ wherever he goes—

Making grace your life's song—

Being buds with the Bible—

Hanging with God's herd.

That's the shot you need to kill the faith-eating bacteria of the cults.

Think About This Stuff:

1. What's the best part of being a cult-proofed Christian?

2. Explain how these five traits boost your immunity to cults:

Know a big God

Cling to Jesus

Glom on to God's grace

Study the Bible

Hang with a herd of other believers

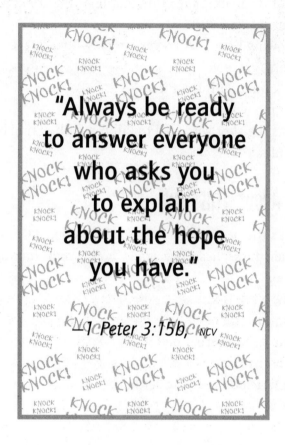

"Always be ready
to answer everyone
who asks you
to explain
about the hope
you have."

—1 Peter 3:15b, NCV

Don't Make Like a Beanbag

chapter **10**

Slide yourself into the shoes of that dude or dudette at your door.

You start by putting on your best clothes—not your *fave* clothes, but the ones your parents make you wear when someone gets married or buried. Definitely a suit and tie. Or a dress cut from Grandma's drapes.

You ding strangers' doorbells.

Maybe you sweat.

Maybe you're so excited you don't.

What happens?

Some people hide. You congratulate yourself, reminding yourself of Bible verses that give you boldness. (" . . . without being frightened in any way by those who oppose you. This is a sign to them that they will be destroyed, but that you will be saved"—Philippians 1:28.)

Some people yell at you. You feel bad, but you get glad. ("Blessed are you when people insult you, persecute you and falsely say all kinds of evil against you because of me. Rejoice and be glad, because great is your reward in heaven"—Matthew 5:11–12.)

Someone joins your church. But some days you hit the jackpot. You're jazzed with joy. ("There will be more rejoicing in heaven over one sinner who repents than over ninety-nine righteous persons who do not need to repent"—Luke 15:7.)

Slide Into Their Shoes

The people at your door die to wear a tie. To knock on doors of people they don't know. To say what they believe even when they'll probably get slammed.

That's one way to measure how much the cults care about their faith—to quantify their sincerity. Sure, some of them go witnessing to rack up points with God. Sure, a few are cultic equivalents of TV evangelists—weirdos always whining for cash. But a lot are everyday people. All they want is for you to know their truth. And they believe God smiles at what they do.

They've got guts. They're way gung-ho.

So how do Christians respond?

There's a *Far Side* cartoon that shows a bunch of beanbags in a living room. As in all *Far Side* cartoons, the beanbags are alive. Out the beanbag family's front window you see two people carrying book bags walk toward the front door. Papa beanbag says to his family, "Look out! The Jehovah's Witnesses are coming! Make like beanbags!"

That's how most folks—including Christians—handle the dudes at their door. Dim the lights. Mute the TV. Make like nobody is home.

Maybe, in a way, nobody *is* home.

In the meantime, these folks—people trapped in false religions, hanging on to false hope that they belong to God, figuring they'll spend eternity with him in heaven—walk by our homes, carrying Bibles and wanting to talk God.

Maybe you witness at school. Maybe you tell people around town about Jesus. Maybe you've even done short-term missions trips. *Don't stop doing those things.* But trudging through your neighborhood, donking your doorbell, these people come right to you. You've got a mission field on your doorstep.

Turn on the lights.

Talk to them.

Catching Up With the Men in Black

What's With the Dudes at the Door? shows you how to spot cults. Describes how cultic beliefs differ from real Christianity. Explains why those differences matter. If you've read this book and discovered the boundaries of your faith—so now you know why and how to stay clear of cultic cliffs—that's great progress. But there's more.

A big hunk of Christians don't like to think bad about anyone. All of us want to be kind. Tolerant. Fair. But being wrong about God carries a high price. Knowing the truth of the true Gospel is heaven-and-hell important.

Paul described people who reject the true God like this: "The god of this age has blinded the minds of unbelievers, so that they cannot see the light of the gospel of the glory of Christ, who is the image of God" (2 Corinthians 4:4). Cults can't see the real Christ. They're blind to God.

That's the need. God has appointed you and other Christians to meet the need: "We do not preach ourselves, but Jesus Christ as Lord, and ourselves as your servants for Jesus' sake. For God, who said, 'Let light shine out of darkness,' made his light shine in our hearts to give us the light of the knowledge of the glory of God in the face of Christ" (2 Corinthians 4:5–6). God put his light in you so you can shine in dark places.

Superheroes Need Not Apply

Countering cults takes courage. But it isn't superhero stuff. You don't blaze over buildings in a single bound. You won't catch bullets with your teeth. There's no chance to pose for admiring crowds, muscles pumped and teeth agrin. Most of all, you can't gallop off on a white horse to single-handedly convert the world from cultism. It won't work. You'll wind up heaved straight over the handlebars of that little ol' horsy. You'll be a real mess if you try.

"Cult evangelism" might sound like raucous fun, but in reality it's a wad of hard work. It's a task you try 1) only with huge caution and study, and 2) only with the help of other Christians. More people than you'd want to think about have gone off on their own to convert cultists and ended up getting converted themselves. Bad move.

A few chapters back you heard about Jude 1:3: Christians follow a "faith once for all entrusted to the saints."

That's the second half of the verse. But now look at the front half. Jude says this: "I felt I had to write and *urge you to contend* for the faith that was once for all entrusted to the saints" (italics added). *Urge* means we may need some prodding. *Contend* means it's a struggle. And get this: Jude says contending for the faith is for all Christians. Two verses back he announced that he was writing "to those who have been called, who are loved by God the Father and kept by Jesus Christ." That's all of us. And to wrap up, Jude tells *why* we need to stick up for what we believe. "For certain men . . . have secretly slipped in among you. They are godless men, who change the grace of our God into a license for immorality and deny Jesus Christ our only Sovereign and Lord" (Jude 1:4).

Assuming you don't want to make like a beanbag, what to do? Do you chump out and say, "Hey, to each his own"? Or do you take a stand for truth and stretch yourself, trusting that God will honor your effort? It can be scary. But then again, some of the coolest things in life are.

Take these five bits of biblical advice on how to talk to the dudes at your door—or wherever you find them. Stick these words of Scripture in your head.

Go Ahead and Get Your Pants in a Bunch

Biggie Truth #1: "Do not participate in the unfruitful deeds of darkness, but instead even expose them" (Ephesians 5:11, NASB).

College students know all about "unfruitful deeds of darkness." Not just buckets of beer or sinful sex—though that's totally dark. The fruit of darkness they know way too well is the stuff that grows in an untended dorm room fridge. Leftovers go in. Door gets shut. Leftovers get forgotten. Door shuts out light. Leftovers start to grow legs.

Get the point: Clean out the fridge, or mold will overtake

everything. Confront the fungus, or it will climb all over you.

So exactly what in life makes you upset? What gets your pants in a bunch?

Worry about too little and you're naïve. Worry about too much and you'll be a crab or a fraidycat. But the wrong beliefs about God should be one thing that bugs you.

Biggie Truth #1 means that exposing evil isn't optional. Responding to churches and organizations that teach falsehoods about who God is and what he's done in Christ isn't a choice any more than letting someone lie about your dad or yo mama or your bestest friend. When someone is *really important* to you—God is, isn't he?—you want the truth to be known about him. You give an answer.

When you care about your faith—and about people—you speak up.

You love *truth*.

You can't tolerate cultists' *faith*.

You have *compassion*.

You also can't tolerate cultists' *fate*.

Exposing evil doesn't mean you drop a brick on somebody's head and then point out the lump to people who pass by. God has other bits of advice on *how* to confront cults. The point of Ephesians 5:11 is that you can't be neutral. God wants Christians to expose and oppose evil, including major religious evil.

Big Hint: Most cultists aren't "evil" in the sense that they *know* they're wrong and deliberately want to drag you down with them. It's their *teaching*—their chucking of God's truth—that is evil. It's their *error* that is without a doubt wrong. But as all those once stuck in cults and then

148

plucked out will tell you, they're really glad God loves evil people enough to deliver them from their errors. It's a good thing: God loves *all* of us "while we were still sinners" (Romans 5:8).

But What Do You Say?

Biggie Truth #2: "But in your hearts set apart Christ as Lord. Always be prepared to give an answer to everyone who asks you to give the reason for the hope that you have. But do this with gentleness and respect" (1 Peter 3:15).

In one verse Peter manages to bundle together a bunch of tips on how to share your faith with anyone. Take a look at each piece:

Make Christ Lord. To "set apart" means "to treat differently" or "to treat as special." The word "Lord" means "master" or "ruler." Your Lord is Head-man. King. President. The Leader. The Boss of All. And your "heart" is the place where you really live, where you make decisions, where you hide your most secret thoughts. So what Peter is saying is this: Down where it really matters, you're to treat Christ in a special way. You're to post a sign that says, "Notice: Christ Is #1 Here." When you make decisions, Christ your Lord should be the first thing you think about. So your whole life—including what you share with unbelievers—should start by remembering "Christ is My Lord."

Be prepared. You won't be ready to counter the cults unless you know your faith—all of it, even the parts adults might think are too complicated for anyone too short to go to seminary. If you love Christ and his Gospel, God's Holy

Spirit *will* teach you his truth. Parts of God's truth *are* tough to grasp, but let the Spirit worry about that. When you give him your willing heart and open mind, it's amazing what he can get inside your skull.

Give answers. There's so much to know about God that you'll be learning for the rest of your life—eternal life, that is. But the *basics* you've learned in this book are your starting point when you talk about God with cult followers. There's no magic formula. But these are the points to get across:

- *God*—There's only one.
- *Jesus*—He's fully God.
- *Holy Spirit*—Believers are empowered by a Holy *he*, not a Holy *it*.
- *Grace*—Salvation is God's total gift to us.
- *Faith*—It's our right response to God's promises, especially the promise of eternal life.
- *Good works*—We live holy lives to say thanks to God, not to win his approval.
- *Bible*—The Bible sums up our faith and doesn't need supplements.

Explain your hope. When you talk to someone caught in a cult, your goal isn't to bash what they believe. Or show how street-wise you are about the cults. It's to pass on the hope we have in Christ.

When you put Christ first in your life, it's going to show. Sure, you might not be the boldest, outgoingest witness ever to walk the earth, but when you love Jesus it *always* shows in some way. Sooner or later you find yourself an-

150

swering questions from people around you like, "Hey, why aren't you scared of the future?" Or "Why aren't you a basket case when things get bad?" Peter says to *always* be ready to explain why you trust God.

Do it gently. Right now our society is afraid to deal with disagreement. It's downright hostile to anyone who claims he's right and others are wrong. But it's intellectually, morally, and spiritually wimpy to ignore big issues and hope for everyone to "just get along." In one way, we *can't* get along with people who lead us into lies.

We don't pick fights. We don't go rude and crude. Instead, we arm ourselves with truth—God's truth—and we fight on the battlefield of ideas. And we do it "with gentleness and reverence." You can't tell folks about how Christ is Lord in your life with your fist. Or with harsh words. Or with anger in your face.

More on that under Biggie Truth #3.

Big Hint: You'll feel stuck when a cultist *agrees* with your explanation of Christian truth—when a Mormon, for example, says, "Yeah, but that's what we believe!" Maybe you *are* digging up the wrong bone. But that's why you need to know your stuff. You don't need to understand every point where every cult errs. But you need to know enough about the cult you're discussing to calmly object and raise questions. When someone pretends to believe just what you do, it's your chance to pop a big "But what about. . . ?" As you learn more about what cults actually teach, you can follow up with pointed questions on how they stray from big Christian truths about God, Jesus, the Bible, etc.

Don't Be a Doof

Biggie Truth #3: "Instead, speaking the truth in love, we will in all things grow up into him who is the Head, that is, Christ" (Ephesians 4:15).

Think about the radical sports fans you know. They paint their bodies in team colors—green and yellow, for example. They dress stupid—ridiculous cheesehead hats. They pay big bucks for tickets—and sit in snowstorms to watch games.

But it doesn't stop there. What do fully focused fans *talk* about all the time? You can't be around them long before they *tell* you who they root for.

So what about Christians? Should people hang around us day in and day out and not know who and what we love? Witnessing isn't spiritual charades where you motion and mime to make your point. Having the truth inside your head doesn't do anyone any good if you don't show it and *speak* it. In the Bible, truth isn't something just to *believe*. It's something you *speak, live*, and *do*. Christians speak up for truth because they love truth, do truth, and live truth.

Paul, though, tells you how to talk minus the obnoxious fan antics. It's a simple formula: *Speak the truth in love*. It's a straightforward balance: *Speak the truth*, but do it *in love*.

If you ever find yourself speaking about Christ in make-people-spew *pushiness* or in make-people-want-to-clobber-you *anger*, you're almost surely in the wrong spot at the wrong time. When you love the people you're talking to, you bend over backward to make things clear to them—and at the same time you don't get bent out of shape when they say something unkind to or about you. They might insult you. Contradict you. Imply you're brainless or evil. If you're speaking the truth in love you'll ignore those zingers and focus on your goal of talking about Christ.

Big Hint: Radical commitment to Jesus doesn't make you beat people over the head with a thousand-pound Bible. In fact, if your zeal isn't directed by wisdom and study it becomes a *detriment to the gospel.* Here's your check: Does your method of sharing Christ move people closer to God? If you mostly make people mad and turn them off to God, you need to rethink your strategy.

Get Some Help!

Biggie Truth #4: "After this the Lord appointed seventy-two others and sent them two by two ahead of him to every town and place where he was about to go" (Luke 10:1).

Quit sweating.

You don't need to know everything.

It's okay to get help. In fact, it's the *only* way to deal with something as difficult as the cults. After all, Jesus taught his disciples to work together. He sent them out two by two. As Jesus shooed his disciples off into the world, he no doubt mumbled something about two heads being better than one.

One of the keys to learning about cults is *learning alongside other Christians.* It keeps you honed, sharp about your own faith, and keen on Jesus. Get smart: It also gives you a headstart. Not a bad idea, considering the libraries' worth of materials churned out by the cults. Lots of smart Christian folks have spent lifetimes studying cult teachings.

And one of the keys to witnessing to cults is *witnessing*

alongside other Christians. You don't have to go to medical school to spot someone who's sick. You notice they need help. You take them to a doctor. The doctor might refer them to a specialist.

Your job? Do *your* part of the job. When you're stumped, you bring the cultist to someone who knows more. That probably means someone at your church.

You're a catalyst. Remember chemistry class? You can put two ingredients together and they just sit there. But the presence of a third chemical makes the mixture do its thing. In this case, you've got a bunch of Christians—your church and others in your area—and your friend the cult member. There's no chemistry between the two until you come along and issue an invitation.

You probably won't get an adult cult follower to come to your church. But it might be the perfect place to invite a friend your age. Not to some hyper Cult Extraction Committee, but to normal stuff—a Bible study, worship, social events. And if your friend says no, you'll see just how seriously your friend—and probably your friend's parents— views your differences in belief.

Big Hint: Pick on someone your own size. Many adults entrenched in cults already can answer your every objection to their beliefs. They're way better prepped than you are. But teens may be questioning their faith and open to hear about yours. Remember this, though: It almost always takes a long time to persuade any cult follower to adopt true faith—just as much time as it takes *any* of us sinners to say "I was wrong."

Get Ready for Some Heat

Biggie Truth #5: "If you were of the world, the world would love its own; but because you are not of the world, but I chose you out of the world, therefore the world hates you" (John 15:19, NASB).

Friendships, relationships, Bible studies, retreats, concerts. Sounds like stuff *we* do. But cults are building these bridges they want *you* to walk over. Bridges with spiritual trolls underneath, for sure. But cultists' evangelism tactics are a lot like ours: Be kind. Show you aren't uncool. Convert all you can.

We're on a collision course. Not because cultists are necessarily nasty. Or crazy. But because at the root of their religions, cults produce unbelievers opposed to God's truth.

You've figured it out by now: Folks who follow cult teachings are—in the vast majority of instances—not Christians. Aside from the rare case of a true Christian who's been deceived for a time, most folks in cults aren't fellow Christians. That includes the nice moral Mormon or the hard-working Jehovah's Witness at school. And that means there's a big spiritual chasm that separates you from that person.

Jesus said that the world—people opposed to God— would *hate* Christians. Ouch. Tough words. God didn't build us to hate. We don't want to be hated. But don't be surprised if you feel heat for opposing cults. Not from all cultists. Not all of the time. But at some point you'll probably face animosity toward what you believe and how you live. You might not see it in open anger, but in cutting comments and mocking attitudes toward your morals and your goals. And if you don't catch it from the cults, you'll hear it from people who think you shouldn't put them down.

Big Hint: Keep showing love even when it's less than fun. Hanging in there even when you feel opposed takes love and dedication. When you love someone you do what's best for them, even tough stuff. Telling the truth to people who've been deceived is never easy. They won't like it, and most non-Christians will think you're slime for sizing up cultists so intolerantly. The world will say you're mean. God says you are doing the right thing. Which will it be?

Hanging With Your Friends

So what happens when your best friend is a member of a cult? It's tough to hear, but you have to limit your relationship to the same kind of friendship you can have with plain old non-religious unbelievers. You can't get "yoked" together to the point that your friend drags you around and causes you to doubt or dismiss your faith (2 Corinthians 6:14–18). Jesus hung out at parties with Israeli IRS agents and odd lots of sinners (Matthew 9:10). But he stood and declared God's kingdom. Somehow he stayed friends. Somehow he got invited back. He was the can't-get-sucked-down-into-sin man.

Most Christians, to be honest, can't handle that—none to the extent that Jesus could. Jesus was powered by prayer. He had fully resolved to do right. And he possessed total knowledge of his Father that made anything else unappealing.

There's a real gulf between you and a friend who's a Mormon or a Jehovah's Witness or anything other than a Christian. Besides that, remember that most cult groups encourage members to get others to join up. Your friend might be trying to get you interested in his or her group just like you want to interest him or her in yours. If you're both committed to what you believe, eventually you'll run head-on into real problems. One possibility? You might have a chance for some meaningful discussions of God's truth. Another possibility? Your relationship won't survive the stress of both of you wanting the conversion of the other.

Git the Door

Getting cult-proofed is a huge job.

Grabbing other people out of cults is even huger.

But God is hugest of all.

Remember David? He was the guy back in chapter 2 who fell for the sweet Mormon girl and finished the story minus both faith and girl.

A similar story with a happier ending: A family calls a cult expert named Peter and begs him to come quick to their house. Their son, Mitch, has fallen for a Mormon cutie. They're actually scared he'll bolt out a window and run away from home—they just had a blow-out about him being baptized in the LDS Church. When Peter arrives they usher him into the living room, and everyone sits to chat. At first Mitch is defensive. But Peter convinces him he's not the boogeyman, and that he really does know his Mormonism. The great news is that Mitch *really* thinks Mormonism is just another Christian church. When Peter presents the facts, he freaks. Mitch wants to believe the *truth*, not a lie. End of story? Mitch faces his LDS lady with the facts, and she drops him. Mitch writes Peter a fan letter thanking him for saving his life. Mitch sticks with the truth.

What the cults teach isn't an acceptable variety of Christian truth.

It's a whole 'nother religion. It sells a whole 'nother god. It leads to a whole 'nother end.

God's truth saves.

You have the truth.

The cults are knocking.

You're the only one who can tuck the truth in your own heart.

You're the only one with your friends who may need to hear the truth.

You're the only one with your front step.

Don't make like a beanbag.

Think About This Stuff:

1. How can you tell that cult members care about their faith? How do Christians usually respond?
2. How do you want to respond next time dudes ding your doorbell? Warning: Are you overeager? What keeps countercult worker wannabes from themselves being sucked into a cult?
3. What five Biggie Truths can prod you to reach out to help people mired in cults?
4. What basic truths should you convey to cultists?
5. What do 1 Peter 3:15 and Ephesians 4:15 say about your attitude as you approach people who follow false teachings?
6. If you have friends who belong to cults, how are you going to share true Christianity with them?

Acknowledgments

From James: Many thanks to my beautiful wife, Kelli. And to my awesome kids, "chunk-off-the-old-block Josh" and Summer, both of whom encouraged me to write something *they* could use in sharing with their friends.

From Kevin: Loads of thanks to my lovely wife, Lyn, for always sticking close. And to my kids—Nate, Karin, and Elise—for being great little friends to us and to each other. Love Jesus always.